# TELLING STORIES

SMITH AND KRAUS PUBLISHERS
CAREER DEVELOPMENT SERIES

FUNDAMENTALS OF ACTING

The Actor's Wheel of Connection by Richard Brestoff

Finding Your Funny Bone: The Actor's Guide to Physical Comedy and Characters
by Nancy Gold

The Great Acting Teachers and Their Methods by Richard Brestoff

The Sanford Meisner Approach Series:

Workbook I An Actor's Workbook by Larry Silverberg

Workbook II Emotional Freedom by Larry Silverberg

Workbook III Tackling the Text by Larry Silverberg

Workbook IV Playing the Part by Larry Silverberg

Toward Mastery: An Acting Class with Nikos Psacharopoulos by Jean Hackett

ADVANCED ACTING

Playing Comedy: A Primer by Jon Jory

Tips: Ideas for Actors by Jon Jory

Tips II: More Ideas for Actors by Jon Jory

They Fight: Classical to Contemporary Stage Fight Scenes by Kyna hamill

Acting Under the Circumstances: Variations on a Theme of Stanislavski, A Step-by-Step
Approach to Playing a Part by Richard Brestoff

PLAYING SHAKESPEARE

Acting in Shakespeare by Robert Cohen

All the Words on Stage: A Complete Pronunciation Dictionary for the Plays of William
Shakespeare by Louis Scheeder and Shane Ann Younts

A Shakespearean Actor Prepares by Adrian Brine with Michael York

PLAYING CHEKHOV

The Actor's Chekhov by Jean Hackett

Contact us toll-free at (888) 282-2881 or visit smithandkraus.com
to order or for more information on our upcoming titles.

# TELLING STORIES

## A GRAND UNIFYING THEORY OF
## ACTING TECHNIQUES

## MARK RAFAEL

CAREER DEVELOPMENT SERIES

SMITH AND KRAUS PUBLISHERS
HANOVER, NEW HAMPSHIRE

A Smith and Kraus Book
Published by Smith and Kraus, Inc.
177 Lyme Road, Hanover, NH 03755
www.SmithandKraus.com

First Edition: February 2008
Manufactured in the United States of America
9 8 7 6 5 4 3 2 1

Book production by Julia Gignoux, Freedom Hill Design
Text design and format by Kate Mueller, Electric Dragon Productions
Cover design by Lisa Rafael Design
Cover photo: Marit Brook-Kothlow and Mark Rafael Truitt in
*Body Familiar*, Magic Theatre, San Francisco, California, 2002.

ISBN: 978-1-57525-565-1
Library of Congress Control Number: 200794260

# CONTENTS

# ❦ INTRODUCTION

In the sixth century BCE in Greece, an event transpired that forever changed the way we view acting. The traditional dramatic form at the time consisted of ritualized choral dances illustrating popular religious and heroic tales. It was a mode of theatrical storytelling. What changed in the sixth century was a revolution of form. Thespis, whose name is now indelibly linked to the profession of acting, broke the mold of accepted practice by separating himself from the narrating chorus. His task now was not simply to relate the events of the story as part of an ensemble, but to portray the hero of that story.

This was not an incidental occurrence. From the earliest tribal gatherings to the epic works of Homer, drama had evolved from a tradition of the storyteller, in which a poet would recount epic myths and themes that defined and instructed his particular culture. The concept of an actor attempting to reveal the subjective life of a character had now been introduced to Western civilization. It was a change in emphasis that would have profound implications that resound to the present day. In that moment, the predominant role of storytelling was usurped by the skills and craft of an individual actor. Later, when Aeschylus introduced a second actor and Sophocles a third, the move away from narrative storytelling and toward enactment and impersonation was made conventional. It is worth noting that in 449 BCE, the first acting competitions were held at the Dionysian festival in Athens in which individual actors were presented with awards. In a relatively short space of time, the way theatre was enacted and was perceived had changed.

What had changed? Some may argue that it was less of a revolution than an evolution, a natural shift in a developing art form. Certainly, stories were still being told, only now utilizing the expression of characters' points of view. However, that shift represented a sea change in how the craft of acting would be approached for the next two millenniums. The ability of an actor to compel and affect an audience through the embodiment of a character would become a quantifiable commodity that would be exalted and rewarded. Some theorists, such as Bertolt Brecht, would argue that focusing on the subjective experience of the character detracts from the message and meaning of the story as a whole. Others, such as Constantin Stanislavski and Michael Chekhov, emphasized the interior experience of the character as a means of deepening and enriching the story being told. The personal and psychological approach was explored and taken to a new level by practitioners such as Lee Strasberg. Sanford Meisner believed the real essence of the story lay not in personal experience but in the moment-to-moment exchanges of the characters as the story unfolds. Modern teachers such as Keith Johnstone focus on the immediacy and directness of spontaneous storytelling through improvisation.

The point of this book is not to choose sides in a debate, but rather to show how all these roads lead to the same desired impact, the sharing of a compelling story with an audience. The events of the twentieth century, from world wars to massive social and political movements and to an increasing fascination with the nature of psychology and the interior life of the individual, have had profound effects on culture. These in turn have impacted the way we construct and tell stories to one another. A myriad of different forms and structures have arisen, some in response to events, some as reactions to each other. If we can look at the context in which these modes arose and understand the evolution of acting as a form, we give ourselves the opportunity to use the means and techniques that have been developed to give ourselves an incredible range of expression that reaches across separate styles and forms. In so doing, we liberate ourselves from the obligation to merely charm and please an audience and instead focus on the story itself and how it informs our work.

One does not have far to look in our own era to see film and television actors being paid millions of dollars on the basis of the relationship they have established with an audience through previous characters they have portrayed. Throughout the centuries, individual actors have assumed a place of prominence in popular culture as they nurtured in audiences powerful associations with the great roles they have played. This is not always a healthy thing. The point of this book, however, is not to ruminate on the vicissitudes of fame and fortune. It is rather to look at the state of the acting profession, and more specifically at the current state of training and preparation for the profession and ask, Is there a better way? Is the enthronement of the individual actor a particularly healthy way to approach the task of conveying compelling drama, or is there an alternative?

Theatre, of all the arts, is the most collaborative of mediums. It requires the efforts of designers, writers, directors, a vast technical staff, as well as actors. In film and television, the number of contributors increases exponentially. Yet the focus on the actors whose efforts so determine the success or failure of the enterprise inevitably distorts the process. Not to sound overly egalitarian, but we are all working at the same job. We are storytellers. It is that simple. All of us who work in theatre or film have a task to achieve, and that is to convey in the most compelling way the story at hand. That seems a blatantly obvious concept. But as I will show, the thorough understanding of that concept and its  application to every aspect to training and performance can have a transforming effect.

# TELLING STORIES

The concept of storytelling as the underlying principle of acting is surely not radical. All theatre and films, for that matter, rely essentially on the transmission of information to an audience. This is not information as in the facts and numbers of a university lecture. Instead, the information contains the situation, the context, the emotional relationships, and the challenges and choices that characters face in the story. Basically, when an audience begins to watch a play, they ask three questions: Who are these people? What is going on? Why do I care? To maintain the audience's interest to the very last moment of the piece, the entire cast and artistic staff must address those needs in the audience.

Too often an actor will begin his work on a text with the question, How can I act this part well? That is fundamentally the wrong question to ask. It is analogous to a plumber being called to fix a sink and asking, How can I use this job as a means to show what a good plumber I am? The customer would be better served if the plumber would simply ask, What needs to be done to fix this sink? That is the very crux of storytelling. It is about focusing on the task at hand. If that plumber facing the broken sink had said, "Not only can I fix the sink. I can re-lay all your underground pipes, modernize your heating system, and put filters on all your faucets," his offers would likely be viewed as at best irrelevant and at worse annoying. So would the actor who views a play as an opportunity to show off his vocal prowess, his imaginative and complex choice-making skills, or his range and virtuosity in developing a character. We would all be better off if he just concentrated on what needs to be done to tell the story to an audience.

Storytelling is an invitation to the actor to pick up her lunch pail, put on her work boots, and join the ranks of workers and craftsmen everywhere. It is also a potential boon to the actor. By embracing the principles of storytelling at the very beginning of the creative process, she avoids many possible pitfalls and much unnecessary work. The goal is efficiency. The framework of the story provides the actor with a context that organizes her choices so that all the efforts become cumulative and move toward the purpose of conveying information. For acting is a constant state of telling. Every movement, every look, every breath taken onstage is a process of revelation and communication. Storytelling affords the actor the means to take control of and the opportunity to take responsibility for that process.

# ❦ 2

# How Did We Get Here?

Theatre in America at the end of the nineteenth century was a popular entertainment form. It was modeled after the continental system of the actor/ manager. Companies were formed around a leading man or leading lady, and the play served as a vehicle for best showing off his or her particular talents. Theatre competed with early vaudeville and minstrel shows for the public's patronage. The tastes ran from broad comedy to romantic and heroic epics. Shakespeare was adapted to these tastes, and the style of performance was in general bombastic and broad. Audiences were not shy about voicing their approval or displeasure. There were some notable original voices in the American theatre as it moved into the twentieth century, among them Eugene O'Neill. Still, the predominant convention remained a star-centered theatre that answered its audiences' need for sensation and escapism. Several thousand miles away in Russia, however, changes were taking place that would transform the American theatre and cinema over the next century.

In June of 1897, Constantin Stanislavski met with Vladimir Nemirovich-Danchenko to discuss what would be his first professional job in the theatre. Stanislavski, whose given name was Alekseyev, had confounded his bourgeois family by acting and directing in the amateur theatres of Moscow. The Moscow Art Theatre (MAT) represented a wholly new endeavor. It was with the passion and conviction of an outsider and the discipline of an accomplished practitioner that he threw himself into the discussion of the burgeoning enterprise. It was decided that Stanislavski would become the artistic director and form the acting ensemble, and Nemirovich-Danchenko would be the literary manager. Stanislavski had been profoundly influenced by recent productions by the Duke of Saxe-Meiningen, the noted German director. The Meiningen Court Theatre used large casts in his historical productions and gave minute attention to detail. Each performer, no matter what the size of his role, had precise functions to perform in a scene. Yet the action was seamless and cohesively orchestrated.

Another major influence on the young Stanislavski was the acting of the Italian tragedian Tomasso Salvini and that of his compatriot, the actress Eleanor Duse. Stanislavski was awed by the passion and intensity of Salvini's Othello and by Duse's simplicity and emotional truth. He wanted to establish an ensemble capable of the precision of Meiningen's troupe with the emotional honesty of Salvini and Duse.

As a performer himself, Stanislavski was acutely aware of the obstacles the actor faced: tension, self-consciousness, and inconsistent concentration among others. He was a diligent analyst of his own creative process, and it was this observational propensity that led him to devise a systematic approach to combat impediments and nurture more truthful performances. Working with his hand-picked ensemble gave him the opportunity to explore approaches and formulate techniques in service of that goal. So began what would become a lifelong pursuit of Stanislavski; the devising and refining of a comprehensive method of training the actor.

Stanislavski understood that plays structurally require a sense of momentum, and that the momentum is fuelled by the contrasting desires of the characters. He saw the *objective* of the character, his innate desire, as his propelling force. That objective then manifests itself in the form of actions—specific expressions of the need to attain the desire. When an action is frustrated, it must be adjusted or replaced by a new action in service to that desire. He called this process *adaptation*. The individual shifts or adjustments are called *beats*. By locating the units in which a character strives for an objective, one can find the score for the entire role. The objective can encompass scenes, whole acts, or the entire play. The largest of these objectives, which defines the life course of the character, he called the *superobjective*. He also used the superobjective in reference to the play as a whole. He saw it as the unifying element, the story as it were, that integrated all the characters' separate actions and objectives and brought them into a satisfying coalescence. He also advocated using "What If?"[1]—a process of investigation by which the actor employs his imagination to gain entry into the *given circumstances,* the facts of the play that determine objectives.

So much of Stanislavski's terminology has entered the popular lexicon that it almost seems cliché. The quotes "One must love art, and not one's self in art" and "There are no small parts, there are only small actors" are his.[2] The *fourth wall* is a concept originally formed by the theorist Diderot to describe an imaginary wall behind which the actors behave as in a private room, oblivious to the presence of the audience. The term was inextricably linked to Stanislavski's naturalist stagings. *Circles of concentration* refers to the means by which an actor anchors his concentration and focuses his attention onstage on objects and activities that absorb him. One of the most controversial aspects of the evolving method was the *memory of emotion* or *affective memory.*

Stanislavski found that to render an intense emotional moment in a play, the actor could look for an analogous feeling that he had experienced in his own life. By revisiting the sensory details of the experience in his imagination, the emotion could be re-created and would therefore be usable in performance. There is an ironic anecdote about these affective memory exercises. Michael Chekhov, one of the most gifted members of the first MAT studio, was doing an exercise in which he recounted the details of his father's funeral. The class and the teacher were profoundly moved, and afterwards Stanislavski embraced the young actor and consoled him. It was only later that Stanislavski learned that Chekhov's father was in fact very much alive. But this is less an indictment of Stanislavski's methodology than it is a reflection of the imaginative facility of the great actor and later teacher, Michael Chekhov.

The critics recognized the evolving style that resulted from these experiments. Still, none of the early productions of the MAT was a great commercial or popular success. However, when the company first assayed the work of Anton Chekhov in their groundbreaking production of *The Seagull,* they found a success and a style that would define them for years to come—naturalism. Naturalism was a style that sought to provide the illusion of actual events transpiring on the stage. Critics and audiences hailed the naturalness and detailed behavior that seemed to emerge directly from each character's subconscious. The MAT found continued success in the rest of Chekhov's canon as well as in the work of Gorky and Turgenev. As the company came to be regarded as the premier theatre in Russia, Stanislavski sought to evolve his methods to produce truthful and compelling acting even in more poetic and symbolic plays such as Maeterlinck's *The Blue Bird* and stylized productions such as *The Marriage of Figaro.* While Stanislavski himself had only measured results in these new forms, under his aegis many of his protégés, such as Vsevolod Meyerhold, Michael Chekhov, and Yevgeny Vakhtangov, successfully pushed his methods into evermore heightened and abstract theatre.

Yet for many, Stanislavski and the MAT would always be associated with naturalism. This was due in part to the manner in which the West was exposed to the work and teachings of Stanislavski. The system that Stanislavski was devising was a revolution in the training of actors. But for those in America, the dissemination of that system was an incredibly slow and inefficient evolution. In 1930 Stanislavski began compiling his notes for a comprehensive book on the system, which was to be called *The Actor's Work on the Self.* When the book was finished, a decision was made to divide it into two parts because of its length. Volume one dealt with the psychological preparation for the role; the second concentrated on the technical and physical aspects. The first volume was published in English in 1936 under the title *An Actor Prepares.* The second volume, *Building a Character,* did not appear until fourteen years later. This led to the misapprehension that Stanislavski's methodology focused exclusively on the psychological at the expense of the physical demands of acting.

Americans gained firsthand knowledge of the work of the MAT in 1923 when members of the company, including Stanislavski, toured the United States. The plays they brought over included Gorky's *The Lower Depths* and Chekhov's *The Cherry Orchard* and *The Three Sisters*, examples of the MAT's mastery of naturalism and ensemble playing. The company consisted of the crème de la crème of Russian theatre, and many of its members, had they not been convinced of the benefits of the ensemble, could have been considered stars in their own rights. The tour created a sensation in the American acting community and led to a hunger for training in this new style of performance. Richard Boleslavsky and Maria Ouspenskaya were members of the first MAT lab who had earlier immigrated to New York during the violent days of the Russian Revolution. They established an acting lab modeled after the MAT and taught a method based on Stanislavski's early work. To their students, the example of the MAT's performances and the teaching of Boleslavsky and Ouspenskaya were a revelation. Lee Strasberg was one of those students. Inspired by the MAT's new approach, he and fellow student Harold Clurman, along with their friend and associate Cheryl Crawford, sought to create an American theatre based on the MAT model. Thus the Group Theatre was born.

In 1931 they formed an acting ensemble culled from fellow students and some of the brightest young actors of the Yiddish and Off Broadway theatre and moved into a farmhouse in Connecticut to prepare. Clurman became the artistic director, Cheryl Crawford would produce, and Lee Strasberg would direct and was placed in charge of training. He based his methods on the principles he had learned from Ouspenskaya and Boleslavsky and on his readings of essays about the system. He emphasized relaxation, concentration, and the use of affective memory. The Group's early productions were appreciated for their truthful intensity and ensemble playing, but their commercial appeal was erratic. It was through the works of the company's resident playwright, Clifford Odets, that the Group found true popular success. With the acclaim of *Waiting for Lefty* and *Awake and Sing*, the Group Theatre became a major force in American theatre. The group almost single-handedly defined a new genre of American social realism by shifting the focus from bourgeois comedy and escapist drama to the sufferings and strivings of the working class.

Yet just as the Group Theatre enjoyed success and an increasing prominence in the American theatre, there were fractures forming behind the scenes. Members of the acting company were expressing frustration over the training methods of Strasberg, specifically, his use of affective memory to achieve truthful emotion onstage. The actors felt that far from creating moment-to-moment life, the technique caused actors to drop out of a scene and create emotion through a kind of self-hypnosis. At this point of crisis, Clurman and his wife, Stella Adler, one of the company's leading actresses, made a sojourn to Paris where they managed to meet with the man who had started it all, Constantin Stanislavski.

Stanislavski was in Paris convalescing from a recent illness. When she met him, Adler told him, "Mr. Stanislavski, I loved the theatre until you came along, and now I hate it!" To which he replied, "Well, then you must come to see me tomorrow."[3] In their sessions together, he explained that his training methods were in a constant process of evolution, and his thoughts on the use and production of emotion onstage had changed considerably. He described to her his method of psycho-physical actions. Stanislavski explained how he found emotions to be elusive and unresponsive to direct manipulation. He found that by committing to a truly expressive physical action suggested by the play's given circumstances, emotion could be evoked indirectly. Adler worked for the next month with Stanislavski and was reinspired by the techniques.

When she and Clurman returned to the Group, she addressed the company with a detailed chart explaining the specifics of the current system as Stanislavski himself had described it. This conflicted sharply with Strasberg, whose methodology was based on the teaching of Boleslavsky as well as on published essays by Stanislavski's colleagues, Vakhtangov and Sudakov describing the system. Strasberg's approach de-emphasized the play's given circumstances in favor of the personal experiences of the actors. He argued that they needn't adhere slavishly to Stanislavski's system, and that, in fact, his own adaptation of the techniques were more appropriate for American actors. This began one of many fissures that would divide the American acting community over the next half century.

The actors saw the new methods as a revelation. Strasberg became increasingly marginalized within the Group as Adler's discoveries became more accepted. However, in spite of the Group's continuing prominence within the theatrical establishment, they never seemed able to use the techniques to expand to a broader repertory outside the plays of psychological realism in which they had scored their first triumphs. They were also undermined by their own success. Three prominent members—Clurman, Elia Kazan, and Robert Lewis—found their directing services much in demand in the competing commercial theatre. Members of the acting company, such as Francis Farmer, John Garfield, and Franchot Tone, heeded the call to Hollywood. Still others discovered a new calling. Stella Adler retired from the stage to teach, eventually opening her own studio and becoming one of the most prominent acting teachers in America. Sanford Meisner, another noted actor in the company, used his experience to devise a wholly different technique of acting. He focused on the moment-to-moment give-and-take of actors in a scene. Through the use of seemingly banal mutual observations and phrase repetitions, he taught actors to discover the essential impulses that allow truthful behavior onstage. He advised his students, "Don't do anything until something makes you do it."[4] His classes at the Neighborhood Playhouse became yet another competing vision for unleashing the actor's potential.

In the coming years, Lee Strasberg would also rise to an unthought-of level of primacy in the world of acting. Kazan had hired him on to teach theatre history at his new Actors Studio. But Strasberg gradually asserted himself as an acting teacher, and his method became the identifying ideal of the studio. These evolving techniques served not only the theatre of the day, which more and more was investigating the subterranean psychology of ordinary people, but also the evolving American cinema. Kazan had scored striking success in both theatre and film with landmark productions such as *A Streetcar Named Desire* and *Death of a Salesman*, and his work had a profound influence on how acting was perceived. American acting aspired to a new level of intimacy that could reveal the deepest emotional truth projected in extreme close up on a 35-millimeter screen. Faced with this daunting prospect, many emerging actors turned to Strasberg's increasingly controversial methods. But there were contrasting choices for young actors seeking to learn the craft.

Michael Chekhov had split with Stanislavski and toured with his own company. He believed Stanislavski's techniques led too readily to a naturalistic style. He emigrated and set up his own studio, teaching a much more physical- and imaginative-based system of training. He advocated establishing the atmosphere of a scene to create the tones of the play, from which the actor could then draw personal inspiration. He also established the use of the *psychological Gesture*.[5] In this technique, the actor physicalizes a character's need or internal dynamic in the form of an external gesture. He then mutes the outward gesture and incorporates it internally, allowing the physical memory to inform the performance on an unconscious level. Much of what Chekhov explored was the question of how to access the unconscious creative self through indirect nonanalytical means. He also taught a range of movement dynamics such as molding, floating, flying, and radiating, which actors could use to find a physical core of a character. His techniques, though seemingly external, were meant to lead the actor to a rich internal life. In spite of his brilliance as an actor and his firsthand experience in the development of the MAT's groundbreaking work, Chekhov as a teacher was overshadowed by his American counterparts and their evolving interpretations of Stanislavski's methods. As if these competing approaches weren't confusing enough, in the early fifties another major influence emerged that brought the entire orthodoxy of actor training into question.

Erwin Piscator was a young director in Germany with a radically different view. He believed theatre needed to forgo the illusionistic tendencies of naturalism and form a direct dialogue with the audience. He believed in a proletarian theatre that spoke to the concerns of the average workingman. Abolishing the notion of the fourth wall, he ushered in a theatre that exposed the means of presentation, using the burgeoning technology of the scientific age to explore themes directly relevant to society. His collaboration with the young playwright Bertolt Brecht laid the basis for a movement in opposition to the Stanislavski-based theatre.

With the rise of Nazis in the thirties, Brecht and Piscator were forced to emigrate. Piscator came to New York where he taught his influential theories at the New School for Social Research, forming an important bridge from the Group Theatre to the evolving acting studios. The Marxist Brecht moved from Austria to the Netherlands to Russia and finally to Hollywood. His most fruitful period came after the end of World War II, when he returned to Germany and led the prestigious Berliner Ensemble. In his plays, he focused on the choices of individuals in the context of larger political and social forces. His characters range from the sympathetic to the grotesque, but all have a recognizable if extremely fallible humanity.

Brecht is largely thought of as presentational because he sought to rid theatre of what he saw as its reliance on empathy and reinforcement of the audience's own moral predisposition. He sought to show the story in a stark unsentimental way. He employed song and broad comedy as a means to distance the audience from emotional identification with the characters. He was a prolific theorist and much has been made of his advocacy of the *Verfrumdungseffect*, or *alienation effect*.[6] In this concept, a role needs to be performed with an objectivity toward the character. The actor works with a consciousness of both the social imperatives operating in the story and an awareness of its impact on the audience as it is told. This may seem to advocate a certain coldness or absence of psychology in the acting. However, Brecht believed in empathy as part of the process of character development. But the character then needs to be contextualized within the story and seen from the standpoint of society.

There seemed a great void between the theatre of Brecht and that of Stanislavski, which was reinforced by Brecht's own diatribes against bourgeois naturalism. But Brecht had little firsthand exposure to the many diverse productions of the MAT and its studios. The critic Eric Bentley best sums up the divergence as such:

> Brecht was a playwright, Stanislavski an actor. For Brecht, actors were the means toward the full realization of his plays. . . . In short, Brecht, who regarded his scripts as forever unfinished, forever transformable, and his dramaturgy as young and developing, tended to regard the actor's craft as given and as already there in finished form. . . . For Stanislavski, on the other hand, it was the play that was a fait accompli. We do not read of his reworking scripts in the manner of Brecht or of the Broadway directors. He was busy reworking the actors. I suppose every director looks for clay to mold. For Stanislavski the clay consisted of actors; for Brecht, of his own collected writings.[7]

So, there we have it. In the course of less than half a century, a veritable explosion of acting theories, each one fighting for primacy as the means to achieve theatrical truth. It is analogous to the schism of the Christian church that arose in the Middle Ages where separate sects and orthodoxies arose vying to be the one true religion and all of them mutually exclusive of each other. How on earth could any actor know which path to choose? Indeed, the choice became even more difficult in the sixties and seventies when movements emerged in response to established methods and practices. Directors such as Jerzy Grotowski in Poland and groups such as the Living Theatre of Julian Beck and Judith Malina and Joseph Chaikin's Open Theatre in America explored a communal, improvisatory process to create an immediate theatre that alternately confronted the audience's preconceptions and invited a more direct level of participation.

If someone was right, was everyone else wrong? If an actor committed to a particular approach, was he then closing the door on a world of possibility? Surely, faced with this Tower of Babel of varying acting theories in the late twentieth century, some rationale would have to arrive. And it did.

# 3

# A New Paradigm Arises

The seventies and eighties saw the emergence of a different notion of actor training, the conservatory program. As the growth of resident theatres throughout the country challenged the primacy of Broadway, so the university-based MFA and certificate programs challenged the New York studio system. Prominent schools such as Juilliard, Yale, New York University, the American Conservatory Theatre, and Carnegie Mellon formed the core of what was known as the League of Professional Theatre Training Programs. These were some of what was at that time, only a handful of conservatory programs. However, when the league disbanded in 1987, it further expanded and decentralized the training process.

In the last twenty years there has been a veritable explosion of MFA programs offered by Universities. These curricula offer comprehensive three- or four-year programs with classes in acting, speech, movement, and theatre history, as well as other subjects such as mask work and stage combat. Most importantly, many are affiliated with professional theatres and offer students a range of performance opportunities. This stands in stark contrast to the New York studios. Despite various efforts, none of the studio-based training schools were able to launch a successful production wing. For many of the actors, the extent of their work on a play involved four- or five-minute monologues or fifteen- or twenty-minute scenes. In a large acting class, students could go weeks without the opportunity to work. While the conservatory programs addressed this deficiency, students were faced with a host of other challenges.

For one thing, the conservatory program requires a level of dedication undreamed of in the studio system. Whereas studio actors could attend a couple of weekly sessions, thereby accommodating their lifestyles, conservatories demand a much more intense level of commitment. Students may need to forgo their apartments, their support jobs, even their personal relationships to invest the three or four years of disciplined work on their craft. After it all, they may be saddled with a mountain of student loans and with no clear prospects of employment. But one of the greatest challenges of the conservatory system is essentially one of aesthetic considerations.

The emphasis on speech, voice, and movement training in the system presents a challenge to the student's notion of self. A typical acting student has spent twenty-some-odd years living in her body and speaking with a particular voice and speech pattern. Her mode of expression represents a unique wealth of life experience—experiences she has obviously drawn on sufficiently well to be accepted in the acting program. Yet from the moment she commences the training, the student is taught to condition and control her particular mode of expression and bring it into alignment with a standard. Clearly, these efforts are intended to enhance and increase the range of expressivity of the actor in service to the work she undertakes.

But a necessary question follows, How do you increase the range and pitch of your ability to interpret dramatic texts, while not losing yourself in the process? Not long ago, I heard an interview with the esteemed English actor, Sir Ian McKellen.[1] In it, he expressed a regret at having worked diligently to remove all trace of his native Lancashire accent. While at Cambridge, he had labored tirelessly to undo the years of personal experience that were reflected in his way of speaking. His own speech pattern was obliterated in order to conform to received pronunciation, the English standard of stage speech. This brings up an important distinction and one that lies at the heart of storytelling.

We must recognize that who the actor is and what he has experienced in his day-to-day life is not necessarily directly applicable or even appropriate to every role he assays. Nonetheless, that underlying self is the foundation for all the work he does in acting. The goal in approaching a role is to form a synthesis, using what is relevant from his own life along with what can only exist in the imagination.

It is a selective process. I certainly don't know what it is to be a king. But I can glean from my life how authority figures deal with those who are subordinate in status. I can understand the weight of responsibility and expectations from my experience. Where I come up short is where my technique and my training in concert with my imagination take over. The purpose of training is not to undermine my sense of self but rather to provide me with a set of tools that enhances all that I am. Truthfully feeling the experience of a character is not enough. One must have the ability to articulate and express that experience to the individuals in the audience, even those sitting in the cheap seats in the back of a fifteen-hundred-seat auditorium. Function must dictate form. We must realize that while getting high marks in speech, voice, and movement does not necessarily produce great acting, neither does exquisitely feeling a role in a performance that does not carry beyond the second row of seats.

The fact is that we stand at an important point in the history of actor training. Great acting certainly wasn't invented by Stanislavski. But the introduction of principles and exercises that increase the expressiveness and impact of actors is a hallmark in the evolution of theatre that stands as one of the greatest artistic breakthroughs of the past century. So many individuals have worked so hard in the development and articulation of specific modes of actor training, that it would be an abomination to turn our back on what has been accomplished. Stanislavski said, "One must give actors various paths."[2]

The challenge is to embrace the divergent paths and put them to work and in service to the ultimate goal, which is telling a story. The key to storytelling is that from the outset the actor must understand that his task is to bring dramatic works to life. Accepting who he is and where he is in his evolution as a human being, he amasses a set of tools. He then uses these tools in service to the range of texts that he seeks to interpret. Just as our aforementioned plumber does not always reach for a wrench on every job he works, so must the actor accumulate a diverse skill set to approach the demands of each job he undertakes. What is necessary is to understand the job at hand. The actor has to know the specific demands of the story being told and how he can invest himself in the process.

# 4

# How It Works

In storytelling, there are two components that comprise the actor's work: the story and the character. They are not separate, however. They are interdependent, and their integration is a key to making a text come alive for an audience. By story I don't mean merely the sequence of events that describes what is happening. Story is not plot. It is multifaceted. The story is all the details and background that give the events a context. It is also the specific relationships between characters that allow events to have importance. But it is more. It is the structure of the telling. By seeing the structure, we understand how a play unfolds and how it is meant to reveal itself to an audience.

That is a simple concept. Anyone can recognize that a comic story is very different in structure and tone from a morality tale, or a mystery, or a tragedy. But getting beneath such simple categorization and into the realm of the mechanics of the story shows us how it is intended to impact an audience. By looking at the story of a play this way, we begin to see it more holistically. We can recognize tones and atmospheres present in the play. We can see tensions and how they move the story forward. Such a process leads us to further questions. If it is a play from classical or modern repertory, what was the story's impact on its original audience? How does its perception change for a contemporary audience? What is still vital about it?

As interpreters of a play, we are in a unique position. We can allow ourselves to be immersed in the world and the details of the story in a subjective way and at the same time stand outside it and see objectively how it will reveal itself to the spectators.

We must bear that in mind when we first pick up a text. Oftentimes we can read a well-known play, and it will still hold many resonances for us. It maintains its ability to make us laugh or move us profoundly. However, there are times an actor can read a play and be left cold. This is when her work truly begins. Leaving aside the fact that aesthetics are not universal and everyone is entitled to his or her own opinion, the actor must ask herself, Am I missing something? The actor must recognize if her own assumptions and preconceptions about a mode or style of drama are preventing her from seeing what is before her.

Plays can't be museum pieces, dioramas preserved behind a glass case. For a play to have survived to modern times, it must have an inherent poignancy and vitality that endures when lesser plays have long been forgotten. We need to look for the humanity, the archetypal themes that allow for a play to be a work of art and not merely a diversion. Even in contemporary scripts, an actor may not immediately find himself in sync with the world of the play, the voice of the writer, or the issues at stake. It is imperative that he keeps looking at all the varied aspects of a play until something sparks his imagination. Whether it is thematic, as in "It's amazing how these characters maintain their dignity and humanity in such adverse circumstances," or more dramaturgical, as in "This play really rips the lid off society's hypocrisy," what is crucial is a point of entry for the actor. His curiosity and imagination need to be provoked so that he can embrace the investigation into the entirety of the story. His work on the story needs to be almost an obsession wherein he familiarizes himself with the specific details of the world of the play, the society it reflects, the structure it utilizes, and the nuances inherent to it. Under all that is his personal connection to the story. Actors don't have to be geniuses. But they need to be curious and possess an empathetic nature that leads them to discoveries.

This work on the story becomes the foundation on which the actor will erect the architecture that his character will then inhabit.

The second major component of storytelling is character. As you will learn in the coming chapters, the means of creating a character and the role of characterization in the interpretation of texts is a subject of much debate. But there is a compass that we can rely on when it comes to character that extends itself across the range of styles and genres. That is the words themselves. Words are the external expression of an underlying meaning. The goal of all characterization is to live inside the words that a character speaks. All characterization has to stem from the actor herself and her own sense of truth. The bottom line is the actor will be speaking these lines in a performance, and she must take ownership of them if the play is to come alive for an audience. But how does she assert such ownership? If she has allowed herself to investigate the fullness of a text in all the aspects that present themselves to her objectively, she has afforded herself a great deal of freedom to explore. She can now focus on the moment-to-moment life of the character as it unfolds through the text.

If we could transcribe any two hours of our conversations and interactions in the course of a day and then read it over, it would offer tremendous insight into our intentions and state of mind. Of course, we would have the benefit of fully knowing the context of each exchange. We would probably be surprised at the variations of thought and associations expressed. While certainly some exchanges are more telling than others, we would nonetheless be able to discover snapshots of our modes of expression. Those snapshots would allow us to see what we choose to say, how we respond to situations, and how we wish to be perceived by those we encounter. There are reasons why we choose the words we do. Our words reflect our desires, our fears, our defenses, our humor, and our ideals. We are social beings, and language is the means we use to participate in society.

The words of a character are no less telling. Not long ago, I participated in a writing workshop with the noted playwright, Arthur Kopit.[1] Twelve playwrights came to the sessions having completed a simple exercise. They had each spent approximately twenty minutes writing a scene. The only stipulation was that each scene begin with the line "Did you bring it?" The "it" is unspecified other than it cannot refer to drugs or sex paraphernalia. As explained by Kopit, that distinction is not for any moral reason but simply because those choices tend to pigeonhole the writers. I was one of four actors who took turns presenting the resulting scenes as cold reads. We of course, tried to read as far into the scene as we could in the fleeting moments after we were handed the scripts, but Kopit was particularly adept at policing these efforts. What these readings revealed was first, the startling variation in theme and tone that the exercise produced in the hands of these gifted playwrights. But for the actors the lessons were more startling. Even without the benefit of analysis and preparation, rich and distinct characterizations emerged. By simply committing to each line and listening to the response, the actors found that the situation, the stakes, and the behavior of the characters were revealed. The scene itself told us how to play it while we were acting.

This in turn told us something about the playwright's process. We as actors tend to view characters as fully formed and conceived in the playwright's mind as he constructs a play. What we found was that the voice of the character and who he is unfolds for the playwright as he writes. The words themselves are clarifying and refining the character for the writer as the play progresses. While playwrights employ different techniques and structures either consciously or innately in their writing, it is important to recognize the process by which the playwright discovers his characters as he writes them.

What this tells us is that by simply verbalizing the script as we read through it, we can gain incredible insights into character. Rather than approaching the play and the character with preconceptions and choices, we need to let the words tell us what to do. An actor needs to discover the character the same way the playwright did. He cannot burden himself with the obligation to get it right or limit himself to a particular emotional score. He needs to test the shape and substance of the dialogue armed with his own particular sense of truth. Only then will he discover the dead ends and the choices that impede the momentum of the character. Using the words as a map will tell him the areas he will need to investigate physically and imaginatively in the rehearsal process. Every time a character refers to a memory or a previous experience, the actor must ground those words in his imagination and make them as tangible as the breakfast he had that morning. The essence of the character is always the words he uses to define himself, and as such it is both a means into, and a constant place to return to, when approaching a character.

These two components, the story and the character form the crux of storytelling. The investigation of each is a search for meaning. The actor has to find personal resonances through each of the components that excite her imagination and ignite her desire to share the story with and audience. It is a simple tenant. If the actor is excited by her work, then she will be exciting to watch. An actor who has not found meaning in these searches is either testing her skills or performing out of obligation. Ask yourself, when was the last time you enjoyed watching someone taking a test or doing a chore?

# ❦ 5

# STORYTELLING AND CHARACTER

While great drama typically makes use of beautiful and complex language, elegantly formulated plot, and powerful themes, its lasting impact is often found in specific characters. By evoking the audience's empathy or challenging its assumptions, by eliciting laughter, rage, or tears, these characters have burned themselves into the collective imagination. Characters such as Falstaff, St. Joan, Faust, Blanche DuBois, Willy Loman, Hedda Gabler, and Hamlet have transcended the confines of entertaining fictions and achieved a status as defining cultural icons.

While there is no questioning the importance of character to the continuing evolution of drama, the question of how to approach a character and the nature of characterization itself is a subject of intense debate among actors, teachers, and theorists. There seems to be an inherent dichotomy in the debate.

*Should a character be created from the outside in or from the inside out?* In other words, ought the actor to establish the character by finding the details and the behavior, the external manifestations of who he is, and then fulfill that form internally? Or instead, are these externals best found as the result of the actor grounding himself in the character's inward mechanisms of desires, hopes, and fears, which then lead inexorably to an outward expression?

*Is building a character a creative or an interpretive task?* Here the question is when an actor approaches a written text, is it just the first step in a creative process? Is her task analogous to a painter who looks at an objective reality such as a landscape or a still life and seeks not merely to represent it but to give expression to her own unique impression of that reality? Or is the proper analogy to a classical musician, who must adhere very strictly to the score he is playing, yet can still find room for interpretation within that structure.

*Is the actor's task to bring himself to the role or the role to himself?* The question here is, What's the nature of characterization? Should the actor seek to mold and transform himself to meet the demands of the character and the world that he inhabits? Or is the actor's charge to personalize the details of the story so as not to violate his own sense of truth. The range of opinions on these questions could not be more diverse.

> The actor does not need to "become" the character. The phrase, in fact, has no meaning. There is no character. There are only lines on a page. They are lines of dialogue meant to be said by the actor. When he or she says them simply, in an attempt to achieve an object more or less like that suggested by the author, the audience sees an illusion of character upon the stage.
>
> —*David Mamet,* True and False[1]

> Transformation—that is what the actor's nature consciously or unconsciously longs for. . . . Every art serves the purpose of discovering and revealing new horizons of life and new facets in human beings. An actor cannot give his audience new revelations by unvaryingly displaying only himself on the stage.
>
> —*Michael Chekhov,* To the Actor[2]

Stanislavski himself was almost obsessive in his analysis of the characters he undertook and his process in interpreting them.

A large part of his methodology is derived from his own attempts to find unique interpretations of characters and then to maintain their internal life in performance. Much of characterization involves the effort to interpret roles that have been played by hundreds, if not thousands of actors previously. But that is not always its sole purpose. Performers such as Eric Bogosian, Anna Deavere Smith, and Danny Hoch have created solo pieces comprised of a diversity of rich and varied characterizations. They take us on a journey into the lives of a range of characters, providing a vast scope of human experience through their own observational and creative skills.

In the face of such a range of opinion and application, how do we best approach the task of characterization within a storytelling context? The answer can be found in the previous sentence. All character depends on context. Both the form of presentation and the specific circumstances of the plays dictate the means by which we approach character. Even in the aforementioned solo pieces, the characters are revealed by virtue of the circumstances to which they are responding. Character does not exist in a void. Rather, it is an essential element to telling a story. In assaying a character, there are a variety of approaches.

## ANALYTIC

This is the approach developed by Stanislavski and refined by American teachers such as Stella Adler and Uta Hagen. In it, the actor focuses on the *given circumstances*, the play's facts and details relating to the character. This in turns allow her to define the *objective*, what the character wants, and the *actions*, what the character does to get what she wants. The actor can also look into the social context of the play to glean modes of behavior and expression. The actor can construct a detailed biography that extends beyond the parameters of the play and personalize details to create a trajectory, an arc of experience within the play. The idea is to establish parameters, a structure if you will, into which the actor can invest her imagination and personal experience.

# TEXTUAL ORTHODOXY

In this approach the sphere of the actor's investigation is restricted to the words characters say and the actions they perform as established by the author. The adherence to that form is crucial. It is applicable not just to works of David Mamet, but to Pinter, Beckett, and Neil LaBute, for example. Character is inherent to the text. Elements such as the rhythm of the exchanges and the characters' intentions take precedence over biography and social context. It doesn't obviate the need for the actor's work. Rather, that work takes place within a tighter focus.

# IMAGINATIVE

This approach is exemplified by the work of Michael Chekhov, Rudolf Laban, Jacques Lecoq, and others. In it, the character is approached through nonintellectual means. Techniques such as changing the physical center and employing different movement dynamics afford an opportunity for the actor to transform his conscious self to fully encompass a character. By invoking his imaginative faculties, the actor is invited to step away from his everyday self into a new mode of behavior and perception. While not completely abandoning analysis and the use of techniques such as objectives, it emphasizes the role of the actor as a creative artist.

# PRESENTATIONAL

In this approach, there is not an absence of characterization. Rather the character, as well as the story as a whole, is presented to the audience without the illusion that events are actually taking place. The analogy is that even as a reader is involved and compelled by a story he is reading, he is aware of the book in his lap. In this form, a character may address the audience and say "This is who I am, this is why am the way I am, and this is what I am going to do," before enlisting in the play's action. This may seem a particularly Brechtian device, but this is exactly what Richard III does at the beginning of Shakespeare's play. While a political or social context can be part of the approach, it doesn't need to be. What this approach does require is a more direct relationship between the actor and the audience.

## OBSERVATIONAL

In this approach, the actor devises a vocabulary of detailed behavior drawn from her own observed experience. Again, it is essentially creative. The actor creates a character by finding revealing details and integrating and elaborating them to form the whole of a character. It need not be literal. An animal or even a machine can provide the basis for a character. While it is most prevalent in the character-driven solo shows, it can also be used in the creation of text-based characters. For example, Laurence Olivier's famous portrayal of Richard III was based in large part on his observations of the theatrical producer Jed Harris.

These approaches need not be mutually exclusive. What is common to them all is the fact that all characterization starts from self. As Uta Hagen stated, "The basic components of the characters we will play are somewhere within ourselves."[3] I was once told by a teacher that all the feelings we will have in our lives we've experienced by age five. This may seem paradoxical when an actor approaches the rage of a murderer or "the pangs of dispriz'd love."[4] But one need only turn to the playground to see the abject terror of a child that thinks she has been abandoned, or the unveiled anger of toddlers fighting over a valued toy. While it is comforting knowing the wellsprings of emotion and behavior that reside within us, it is a different task altogether to access them through our conscious creative self. How do we marry the actor's subjective experience to the demands of an objective form? For character is an objective portrayal. While the text gives us the words and actions, it is not enough. It is through the three-dimensional living portrait, shared with an audience, that drama actually takes place. Actors look for a telling gesture, a glance, the chance revelation that can give a character a flesh-and-blood humanity that serves the written text and yet, enhances and reinforces it.

As a means of bridging the subjective to the objective, we need to envision a triangle. One corner is the actor himself with all his subjective insights and creative faculties. The next corner is the character as dictated by the story being told. The third corner is the audience, the perceivers of the character in the context of the story. The actor's task is to construct the character with the contingent factor of how that character is received by the spectators. As we have said, everything done onstage is an instruction to the audience's understanding. Within the context of storytelling, the actor must take into account how his conception of the character affects the understanding of the play as a whole.

This triangular relationship exists from the first rehearsal through the run of the play. In the earliest stages, the director serves the role as surrogate for the audience, modulating the performance and maintaining as a whole the disparate aspects of the character. In performance, the actor can continue to subtly adjust the characterization based on the reactions of the audience while maintaining the established form of the play. If any one leg of the triangle is neglected, the whole suffers. If the actor refrains from the use of herself, the character becomes a mere collection of mannerisms devoid of a human face. If she relies solely on herself, the character will lack the scope and specificity that the story requires. If she neglects the audience, the role will lack the meaning and breadth that assures its impact.

So far we've focused on the variety of forms of characterization. But as we've stated, in a storytelling model, the challenge is to find the practical means to sharing the story. The important link between story and character is formed by first understanding the structure of the story, and then by exploring a range of approaches that will allow the actor to invest his energy and artistry in service to that structure. By doing so, the actor can work efficiently, and his process can be tailored to the task at hand.

# 6

# THE STRUCTURE OF THE STORY

We live in the most story-oriented culture in the history of the world. Think about it. Every day in America, hundreds of stories are beamed through the air or travel through cables to television sets in the living rooms of millions of households. In the midst of these comic or dramatic stories are interspersed thirty-second or one-minute narratives that reveal the plight of a housewife or a lonely, single, or frustrated consumer who faced with an intractable dilemma finds the solution in the form of a detergent, a beer, or some other consumer product that we too are encouraged to purchase. The longer stories compete with sporting events and so-called reality shows whose appeal to viewers lie in the fact that they are stories with indeterminate endings. There are also music videos, which have the unique allure of being a musical narrative married to a visual story. Video games have evolved to the point of being interactive stories with hundreds if not thousands of possible outcomes. If we actually want to leave our houses we can go to a movie, a play, an opera, a ballet, or just to the video store, where again we can encounter thousands of choices of stories in the form of videos and DVDs. Then, of course, we still have books and magazines and even newspapers and television news wherein journalists seek to take objective facts and compile them in the form of stories that can capture and hold our interest. In fact, in America in the twenty-first century, storytelling never ends.

What then are the repercussions for those of us whose essential form of expression is the telling of stories? It's daunting. By overwhelming the audience with stories, we have educated them—not in the conventional sense, but in the ways and forms of storytelling. As a result, audiences receive and process information at an incredible rate. This ability, however, is coupled with impatience and skepticism of the process. For centuries, playwrights have used specific structures and techniques to veil their intentions and manipulate and focus the audience's attention in a sort of sleight of hand. But the audience is on to the trick.

Today we are faced with three alternatives: (1) The audience gets ahead of the story, anticipating actions and events. As a result, the audience's interest wanes. They get restless and bored. (2) The story gets ahead of the audience. Either the narrative or the structure confounds the audience's attempts at understanding. They become frustrated, alienated, and ultimately bored. (3) The unfolding story and the actors' efforts work in harmony upon the audience, creating an immediate moment-to-moment experience. The spectators' attention remains focused until the last possible moment of the story.

Obviously, we're shooting for number 3. But the question is how do we get there? Acting with a great passion, sensitivity, and sense of truth is necessary but not sufficient for achieving the task. One must also understand the means the playwrights have employed to tell the story to an audience. Actors can then focus and modulate their efforts in service to those mechanisms. By doing so, the actors' work becomes simpler because the task becomes better defined. Structure becomes a medium through which the actor can invest all his creativity, sensitivity, and technique.

It is perhaps best to look at drama itself as a language, a means of communication. Structure then forms the grammar of plays, and the techniques used within the structure are the vocabulary. To convey meaning, we require form. No idea, concept, or insight can be expressed without it. Both the speaking and the comprehending are a matter of mutual agreement. So is the relationship between the storyteller and the audience.[1]

## ACTION STRUCTURE

The important thing to realize is that there is no one structure in drama. There is, in fact, a myriad of structures. Sometimes they stand alone, and at other times, they are interwoven. The primary structure we find is *action structure*. Roughly 90 percent of all plays are written in this form. It is a prejudice handed down from *Poetics*, Aristotle's analysis of classical Greek drama. It has nothing to do with physical activity. Rather, we need to think of action as change, an intrusion. In this form, a flow of events is presented, establishing the world and characters of the play. The action then intrudes on the flow of events, forcing change. In Aristotle's model, the change is to the direct opposite. He advocates as much change in scenes, characters, and events as is possible. Such change is called a *reversal*. The reversal represents a frustration of the audience's expectations and is a key to dramatic structure. In classic action structure, there is one major reversal in a play. This comes typically in the form of a discovery, which forces a change of perspective in the characters. The discovery can be of a fact, a previous event, or of a relationship to another character. It constitutes the middle part of the action structure.

1. Beginning: the flow of events is established
2. Middle: the reversal interrupts the flow
3. End: a resolution is found

There are three alternatives that can form the resolution: (1) The flow of events is stopped; (2) the intrusion palpably disappears; or (3) a stalemate becomes permanent.

This may seem overly technical, so let's take an example of an action structure: A young married woman, who has been living in a world that betrays her integrity, *discovers* the falseness of her life and *decides* to go. Those familiar with the work of Henrik Ibsen will recognize the essential structure of *A Doll House*. Action structure should fit into one sentence: subject and predicate. The predicate or verb is the hinge. The discovery forces the resolution, which comes in the form of a decision. As a result of the initial situation, the verb reverses the situation.

All the characters have actions that serve a function in relation to the main action. They can help to establish the situation, they can be vehicles for the discovery/reversal, or they can combat or assist the resolution. In this way, the action defines character. Any past outside the structure is irrelevant. There needs to be just enough background information to make them viable proponents or opponents to the central action. The audience then imputes the past. In the spectators' imagination, they encompass the details and events that have led the characters to this crucial point, literally filling in the blanks.

The whole point of the structure is to draw the spectators into the story and maintain their involvement. The audience is engaged by the frustration of their initial expectations, by the tension in anticipation of either the discovery/reversal or its impact on the characters, and finally by the satisfaction of their need for resolution. In response to this structure, writers over the past fifty years have elongated the line of anticipation of the reversal in order to amplify the tension. Samuel Beckett and Eugene Ionesco, in fact, proceed and conclude plays without any reversal whatsoever, frustrating the expectations of an audience conditioned to the action structure.

## RETROGRESSIVE ACTION STRUCTURE

As I stated, in a classical model, the structure hinges on a discovery that reverses the present flow of events. What happens when a series of discoveries lead to the major reversal? This forms what is known as a *retrogressive action structure*. The story moves backward, thereby filling in the audience's and/or the characters' understanding of events. Yet the action moves forward. In this way, the audience is enlisted in the investigation of what caused this series of events.

The classic example of a retrogressive action is Sophocle's *Oedipus Rex*. In the play, Oedipus, the king of Thebes, is confronted by a plague that has descended upon his country. He learns that an oracle has proclaimed that the plague will end when the former king's murderer is found and punished. As Oedipus searches to find the murderer, a series of revelations unveil the truth of his own birth and upbringing. He is forced to confront the final realization that he, himself, is the murderer, and the widowed queen he married is actually his own mother. In response to this last major discovery, Oedipus blinds himself in penance and departs to a self-imposed exile. The ordered present at the play's beginning is gradually undone as the past is discovered. Every fact of the past revealed triggers and action. The key is revelation. The structure, the ordering of events, gives the audience the criteria with which to judge.

It is crucial in this structure for the writer to have a late point of attack, relatively close to the reversal itself. Henry James writing in the nineteenth century described plot as a long tunnel in which the past is foreshortened. The emphasis is always on the present, but the past illuminates and changes the dynamics. Playwrights throughout history have adapted this retrogressive action structure. Ibsen used the structure well and often. Sam Shepard's *Buried Child* is purely retrogressive. The truth on which the entire action hinges comes at the last possible moment onstage. In contrast, Shakespeare's episodic structure has an early point of attack. He introduces characters and action to develop momentum toward a climax without inquiring into the past. The retrogressive structure works almost as a detective story, directly investigating the past in order to make sense of the present.

## MODEL FORMS

In the nineteenth century, action structure led to the development and use of *model forms*: the *well-made play* and *melodrama*. These structures require the tracking and shaping of the audience's response. In melodrama, music would literally cue the emotional response. The practice was to excite the audience to a level of anxiety called *suspense*. The spectators must empathize with at least one character. Instant empathy combined with overwhelming obstacles creates suspense. The use of mounting reversals and discoveries build anxiety, which crescendos at the curtain of each act. The principle of pleasure being primarily composed by tension and release is fundamental to these forms. Complications lead to a climax, which demands a resolution. The finale is the highest possible tension and the highest possible release.

Many well-made plays portrayed the complications and entanglements of the bourgeois society, which formed the core of the play's audience. This allowed for an identification and empathy that could draw the spectators through the series of discoveries and crises to the inevitable happy and neatly resolved ending. By contrast, much melodrama took as its subjects the lower classes of society and heightened domestic situations to nightmare proportions. Moral and social themes were introduced, and the triumph of the protagonist at the play's end represented a confirmation of the social order. This established melodrama as an entertainment form for the proletariat. Both these forms have survived today in plays, film, and episodic television. Now, however, instead of complications and tension building to the curtain falling on an act, they build to a commercial break.

## OTHER STRUCTURES

While many playwrights relied on these conventions, many others reacted against the artificiality and manipulation inherent in them and sought out new forms. Some turned to symbolism and metaphor, abstractions of structure. Others looked to alternative structures. As we stated earlier, the action structures described constitute roughly 90 percent of written drama. But there are other recognizable structures that have been adapted and utilized throughout the evolution of theatre.

## PROCESS

*Process* is a time continuity in which something is accomplished. It has a structural formality. A clear example is the English playwright David Storey's *The Changing Room*. The entire play transpires in the locker room during the course of a rugby match. The purpose of the structure is to mask the internal dynamics of the characters with a common task that veils the action. Process confirms the reality to the audience. They are hypnotized, in a sense, by the desire to see the outcome of the process. The continuity is of an activity and is not punctuated by reversals as in a traditional action structure.

Anton Chekhov used process often in conjunction with his characters' internal action. In *The Three Sisters*, it forms a double structure. The second act is dominated by the activity of a party being organized and then falling apart. Act three is governed by the reaction to a fire in town and the finding of accommodations for the victims. The final act is a series of farewells, preparing for the departure of the regiment. Creating this specific external reality masks and at the same time reinforces the internal dynamic of the individual characters.

## RITUAL

*Ritual* is a form that provides an alternative structure to a play, giving a story a dimension that it does not have on its own. It creates in the audience a sense of a lasting impact, a hugeness of reference. In *Tooth of Crime*, Sam Shepard transfers classical Greek elements of action and ritual to the contemporary arena of rock and roll. In *Angels in America*, parts one and two, one of Tony Kushner's major plot lines is the calling of a prophet. It provides the plays with a scope and metaphysical resonance that transcend the immediate interactions of the characters. Ritual is a formalized activity with symbolic and reverential overtones, although it need not subscribe to any particular religious orthodoxy. It can also incorporate elements of primitive ritual—the rights of passage, the journey of a shaman figure, the trials of a hero who must redeem and heal the body politic. Many playwrights have returned to classical motifs to investigate these larger themes. Jean Cocteau did so in *Orpheus* and *Antigone,* as did Jean Paul Sartre in *The Flies*, his retelling of Aeschylus's *The Eumenides.*

## CEREMONY

*Ceremony* is a formal process in which the participants are conscious of and adhere to a predetermined set of rules. Yet ceremony possesses little or none of the reverential overtones found in ritual. It is utilized in trial scenes and interrogations. Its formalized conventions provide a context from which the characters' individual actions can arise. Ceremony can be used in entire plays, such as *Twelve Angry Men* or *A Few Good Men*, or in specific scenes. However, the rules themselves need not be as formalized as a court proceeding. Ceremony can be domesticated. Mutual social interaction can become ceremony. Harold Pinter uses a bowl of cornflakes in *The Birthday Party* to reveal an intricate family ceremony. Similarly, many characters in Samuel Beckett's plays employ ceremonies to fend off the terrors of existential crisis that dwell just below the surface of their conscious behavior. In this way, ceremony can become compulsive, a means of marking time without moving any discernible action forward. It differs from *process* in that process represents a finite time continuum of activity. It is a straight line of accomplishment. Ceremony can be thought of more as a circle that surrounds and dictates the behavior of those contained within it.

# TECHNIQUES
## TENSION OF OPPOSITES

These structures form the skeletal frame of the story. The muscle and tissue that animates it can be found in the techniques that playwrights employ. The major technique used in drama is the *tension of opposites*. It applies not just to the entire structure, but also to individual scenes and moments and to the characters themselves. It is, in essence, an antidote to boredom. Lack of tension produces stasis, a loss of momentum that is fatal to dramatic storytelling.

As it applies to character, lack of tension can be summed up in the principle: sameness equals dullness. If a character remains consistent, he has no life. He only becomes interesting when he is balanced between competing characteristics. If he defies a definition based on traits, he becomes a person. Don Quixote, for example, is both a saint and a fool. Likewise, there can be *tension of motive*. Hamlet needs to revenge his father's murder and yet doesn't want to be defined merely as a revenger. It is a balance of absolute opposites that compels us as an audience. There is a danger, though. If the tension is too extreme, the character can become comic and descend into self-parody.

The idea that characters must change through the story is a twentieth-century delusion. Rather, the character must be seen in a multiplicity of ways. Once again, the key is in the revelation. What is important to the storyline is the increasing understanding of the character by the audience, not an external progression from one trait to another. In Arthur Miller's *Death of a Salesman*, there is an unexplained anger and bitterness that colors the relationship between the characters of Biff and his father, Willy Loman. An event from the past, revealed late in the play, clarifies the reasons for the split and motivates their behavior in the present tense. Actors often look for cohesion, for an underlying core that can explain the disparity of a character's behaviors. In fact, all restriction on the range of emotion and life that can be represented theatrically is essentially false. The discontinuity is the essence of the role. The spectator infers the wholeness of the character. It is the same principle found in Pointillism, Impressionism, or in our own digital age of pixilated images. Close up, the portrait is blurred and incomprehensible, but given distance, these diverse elements create an impression of a whole. Like that broader canvas, the context of the story allows the audience to perceive the multidimensionality of the character.

Tension of opposites can be used in a multiplicity of ways within the structure of a play.

## Setting Versus the Characters' State of Being

In this use, the external atmosphere is put into opposition against a character's inner state. The contrast emphasizes and amplifies both states. Shakespeare uses this in *Macbeth* in contrasting the jovial formality in the beginning of the banquet scene against Macbeth's burgeoning paranoia.

## Style Versus Content

*Style versus content* is a tension of form. Jean Racine, for example, juxtaposes the extreme agony of his characters' expression within an extremely delicate verse line.

## Tension of Opposites within the Structure of a Scene

A loves B, B loves C, B is indifferent to A. This describes the relationship between Trepliev, Nina, and Trigorin, respectively, in the second act of Anton Chekhov's *The Seagull*. Our understanding of the characters' internal states creates an exquisite and tangible tension. Chekhov was, in fact, a master of the use of tension of opposites, often employing two tones in conflict with each other. At the end of *The Seagull*, we witness a group of card players onstage calmly engaged in a game of lotto, while offstage the despondent Trepliev fires a bullet into his brain. These tones are not reconciled at the play's end, leaving the audience in a state of aesthetic suspense. Chekhov continually employs a number of different tones, all in conflict with one another. By maintaining these separate tones and renouncing the classic action structure in which all stage events build to one neatly constructed climax, Chekhov creates something more ambiguous and ultimately more like life itself.

These uses of tension are not the overt form of manipulation found in melodrama. Rather, they inform an audience on an unconscious level and draw them into the action based on the innate desire for resolution of a conflict.

# GAPPING

Another widely used technique in drama is that of *gapping*. As character is hurt by consistency, storytelling is hurt by being continuous. The essence of the technique is to be discontinuous. It is hard to perceive because the audience fills in the gaps and creates the moment-to-moment experience. Yet it is essential to maintaining the audience's interest and is a means of activating the audience. An example is Jan de Hartog's 1952 play *The Four Poster*. In it, years pass between scenes, and yet there is no direct exposition of the continuing life of the characters. It is merely implied. The spectators fill in the gaps based on the characters' behavior in the present and the audience's common human experience and understanding.

## Time Gaps

*Time gaps* represent the most elementary form in playwriting. In it the investigation of events is restricted to a necessarily narrow focus. The present behavior of the characters gives insight into events. Passage of time is implied.

## Subject Matter Gapping

*Subject matter gapping* is another more subtle technique. In it the relationship between characters is revealed by indirect means. For example, a glass of water in Harold Pinter's *The Homecoming* defines the status and power struggle between characters.

## Gapping the Reversal

*Gapping the reversal* is a technique in direct contrast to action structure. The reversal is approached and then omitted. Only the consequence of the reversal is revealed. Again in Pinter's *The Homecoming*, the major event of the play is not overtly disclosed. Rather, through the behavior of the characters, we infer the nature of the incident and its psychological impact. Pinter is a master of gapping, often omitting direct exposition and relying entirely on characters' actions to tell the story. In approaching the work of Pinter, it is not the actor's responsibility to create the consistency behind the text, for it destroys the mystery. Instead, he must play each unrelated segment with a total commitment to what the characters do.

Gapping events is a way of muting the musical structure of a play. Events transpire, but they are not revealed overtly. Again, we return to Chekhov. In *The Three Sisters*, the fact that Natasha's children have been sired not by her husband but by her paramour Protopopov is merely implied. Yet, it is a seminal plot point. The rules of nineteenth-century playwriting dictate that discoveries and reversals build to a climax. However, by omitting the discoveries themselves, the playwright focuses the audience's attention on their impact on the characters. We then interpret the behavior with a new knowledge of the events.

## DIFFUSING THE CLIMAX

*Diffusing the climax* is a means of obscuring the central focus of the play. In a conventional presentation, the reversals are highlighted, built up to, and focused on, leading to a central climax. For example, all the events in Shakespeare's *Othello* form a pyramid, its apex being the image of Othello's hand holding the dagger. Yet in the twentieth century, we see a dispersal of this hierarchy of focus, which creates a multitude of tonalities at the play's climax. At the end of *The Three Sisters*, there are five separate foci, all with separate tones: (1) The sisters bound together. (2) The military band playing in the distance. (3) Andrei walking alone with the pram. (4) The doctor Chebutykin alone amidst his own despair. (5) The schoolmaster Kulygin perfectly happy, as if none of the preceding events had transpired, waiting to take his wife Masha home.

The use of two separate foci is not as rare. A vast difference of tone is what disperses the focus. It creates a sense of separate finalities. At the end of William Inge's *Bus Stop*, the departure of Bo and Cherry to start their lives together is contrasted with the image of Bo's friend Virgil left to face an uncertain future alone. This creates in the audience a sense of characters' lives continuing past the central climax of the play.

## Zero Ending

Playwrights such as Samuel Beckett have taken this technique even further to the notion of *zero ending*. In this practice, the play ends without any climax whatsoever. This creates in the audience a sense of arbitrariness, the possibility that the events witnessed are part of a continuum that exists before and beyond the spectators' ability to witness them.

Even as you read these words, writers are embracing these structures and techniques or are confronting them in a search for new means with which to engage an audience. For drama is in a constant state of evolution, at once embracing its past and reacting against it in an effort to weave stories out of our shared experience.

But an actor might easily ask why? Why do I need to understand and engage in these underlying principles? Isn't that the province of directors and academics? Isn't the actor's task to explore and commit to the characters and the words they express? To this I reply: Is a painter made more or less of an artist by his understanding of the laws of perspective and the rules of light and shadow? Is a surgeon undermined by his grasp of the workings of the body at a cellular level and the chemical reactions that govern its functions? Great actors recognize the structure of the story unconsciously, and it has become an innate part of their process. The challenge for us then is to analyze and understand structure consciously so that it informs our work and clarifies our choices at the outset. Richard Feynman, the Nobel Prize–winning physicist, had an apt reflection on the subject:

> I have a friend who's an artist and he sometimes takes a view which I don't agree with. He'll hold up a flower and say "Look how beautiful it is. But you, as a scientist take it all apart and it becomes dull." I think he's kind of nutty.
>
> First of all, the beauty that he sees is available to other people—and to me too, I believe. Although I might not be as refined

aesthetically as he is, I can appreciate the beauty of a flower. But at the same time I see much more in the flower than he sees. I can imagine the cells inside, which also have beauty. There's beauty not just at the dimension of one centimeter. There's also beauty at a smaller dimension.

There are complicated actions of the cells, and other processes. The fact that the colors in the flower have evolved in order to attract insects to pollinate is interesting; that means insects can see the colors. That adds a question: does this aesthetic sense we have also exist in lower forms of life? There are all kinds of interesting questions that come from the knowledge of science which only add to the excitement and mystery of a flower. It only adds. I don't see how it subtracts.[2]

In anatomizing the structure of drama, we only add to its beauty and to our own understanding of that beauty. Our next task is to explore the specific means to reveal that beauty to an audience.

# 7

# In Class

aving explored the context and structure of storytelling, we are now free to investigate the tools that are at the actor's disposal. The emphasis is on process and playing. This chapter begins with many games. The idea is to instill a sense of fun and playfulness that concretizes the concepts while at the same time disposing of inhibitions. Even the exercises that demonstrate specific techniques need to be approached not as work, but as something pleasurable. Actors need to understand the purpose of the techniques, but they also need to discover their uses through playing.

An acting class is a laboratory. Within the confines of its walls, a safe and nurturing environment needs to be established. It is a place for actors to try and, most likely, at times to fail. But growth and learning can't occur without the willingness to risk. The work is collective and cumulative. Every actor's success in even the simplest task can inform and inspire the group as a whole. The goal for a student should not to be to become a great or even a good actor. Such assessments are irrelevant. The purpose must be to explore and experience the means of effectively sharing a story with an audience. Any actor who shines in a given moment has not profited by the experience if he cannot understand consciously what allowed that moment to happen.

All students must be discriminating. No teacher can hope to

fully understand the internal processes at work inside each student. This requires the student to be constantly investigating and testing every aspect of the training in respect to her own particular point of view. Students can never afford to check their personalities and subjective selves at the door of an acting class. In many ways, the actor's own judgment will provide the compass with which to navigate through all the material presented. Coupled with this understanding, however, must be the knowledge that without committing and fully enlisting in the process, they cannot hope to arrive at an approach toward acting that works for them. Actors must be prepared to feel uncomfortable at times and to exist in a state where behavior and how we control it is the subject of investigation. As in a scientific laboratory, they should realize that there are no predetermined outcomes, but that the possibility exists for increased knowledge and for finding the means to maximize our impact on an audience. The objective of an acting class is not to transform each student into some preconceived notion of what an actor is and what an actor does. Instead, it is a process of empowering them by providing the tools to establish a connection to the material and to use that link to share the story with the audience.

# STARTING OFF

## DIALOGUE

One of the most important aspects of the training is the establishment of a dialogue. I find a simple conversation is often the best way to start. It provides a means to explore the concept of acting as storytelling as well as its inherent vocabulary. But more importantly, it provides the opportunity for the students to express who they are and where they are in the process. What are their assumptions and preconceptions? What are their fears? What do they perceive as the obstacles to acting well? What do they find most deadly onstage? Questions should always be formed in such as a way as to elicit opinions and beliefs and without the onus of there being a "correct" answer. By sharing in the context of a dialogue, they give voice to what is an essential component of their training, their own judgment. It is also an opportunity to establish the safety and trust of the laboratory environment. While it is necessary for actors to be discerning and maintain a healthy skepticism regarding the processes in which they will be enlisted, they need to refrain from being judgmental toward one another. The final arbiter of each actor's progress will always be the instructor, and students need to know that they are surrounded by collaborators and not by critics. This dialogue must be established and returned to at several points in the process as a means of digesting and assessing the material covered.

## CIRCLE GAMES

The purpose of the early exercises is to dissolve the reservations of the students and establish a working ensemble. The exercises are by nature simpler and less focused than the later improvisation exercises. Both the games and the warm-up are undertaken in a circle with actors standing a few feet apart from one another.

### The Name Game

Everyone states his or her name in clockwise order moving around the circle. They repeat the process three times and then reverse direction and state their names one final time. When everyone, including the instructor, has a reasonable chance of remembering each other's names, the game begins. The first player makes eye contact with someone in the circle and states the other player's name. If it is correct, that person nods, giving the first player permission to come and take that second player's position in the circle. As player one crosses the space, player two makes eye contact and names someone else in the circle. If he gets the name right, he gets a nod and moves across the circle. No player is allowed to move until she has received a nod. In the beginning, players should be encouraged to aid their fellow students. At first the game should proceed slowly and mistakes are forgiven. However, after a few dry runs, it becomes more competitive. Speed should be enforced with no hemming or hawing.

The game ends when a student volunteer names everyone in the circle. This game emphasizes observation and concentration, but most of all it serves the practical function of introducing class members to one another.

## Zib Zab Zoob

Players stand shoulder-width apart in the circle. The starting player simultaneously claps and points his clapped hands either to the right or left. If he points to the right, he says *zib*, to the left, *zab*. The player who receives either the *zib* or the *zab* is then faced with the same choice. She can either return a *zib* as a *zab* or keep it going around the circle as a *zib*.

It is a good idea to work with just *zib* and *zab* at first. Once these terms have been practiced, you can add *zoob*. *Zoob* is a block. A player can clap his hands over his head and say *zoob*. This forces the previous player to change her direction. However, you can't *zoob* twice in a row. The game should start slowly with the goal of achieving a very high rate of speed. When a player makes a mistake, he must take the "seat of shame" and sit on the floor. The standing players continue until only a handful remain. Through it all, it is important to maintain a sense of playfulness and goodwill.

Once this round has been mastered, more or less, it's time to graduate to its advanced versions. In one version, the game is played nonverbally, with the claps alone determining direction. This round is particularly exciting when played at breakneck speed. In another version, *zib* is replaced by *hi*, *zab* by *what?*, and *zoob* by *stop!* With the addition of dialogue, the clapping is abandoned. This complicates what is essentially a game of reflexes by adding familiar conversational interactions. Almost immediately the players are thrown by the engagement of the cues as their brains have to process on a less technical level. As a result, the game also becomes more fun to watch and play. The play proceeds in the same fashion with players who make mistakes taking the "seat of shame" and the circle tightening.

When players have had a fair crack at this version, it's time to move on to the final incarnation. In this version, *hi* is replaced by *I love you*, *what?* by *I hate you*, and *stop!* by *back off!* The game now devolves to the ridiculous, and the benefit is watching the distance between players dissipate as they embrace the intention of the phrases. This round is genuinely fun to play and is usually the last form. However, after a few go's, the instructor has the option of offering a further variation. In this, players play by the same rules, but the intentions are reversed so that when they say "I love you" they mean "I hate you" and when they say "I hate you" they mean "I love you." This adds another level to the game as players learn to play opposites and mask intentions.

## Circle Mash

This game requires a fair amount of space, as it is quite physical. Players stand in a circle with one player in the center. As the center player surveys the group, any two players in the periphery make eye contact, which serves as a nonverbal agreement to trade positions in the circle. The object for the center player is to occupy one of the vacated spaces before the switch is successful. If he or she does so, the stranded player assumes the center position and the rest of the players continue to seek out partners for switches. The game stresses the potential for nonverbal communication. The danger is in the near collisions that may result during switches, and it is imperative that the instructor stresses safety and that players remain diligently aware of their physical selves in the space.

## Rhythm Circle

In this game, players form a circle and one player is sent out of the room. The instructor then selects a leader by means of a simple pat on the head. The leader then initiates a rhythm pattern by patting various parts of his body with his hands. The group mirrors the leader's actions. The first player is then led back into the room and must guess the leader as the rhythm changes. The goal of the leader and the group is to constantly vary the rhythm, patting different body parts, without giving away the leader's identity. Depending on the size of the group, the player gets two or three guesses to ascertain the leader. The goal is to find the leader as quickly as possible.

The instructor should time the guesses to see which player is most adept at the task. This is another game that emphasizes observation and nonverbal skills.

## Pat

This game was introduced to me by friends who had studied the methods of Jacques Lecoq. In it, students sit in a circle cross-legged with knees touching. The players then place their right hands on the left knees of the player to the right and their left hands on the right knees of the players to the left, so that every player in the circle has each hand resting on another player's knee. The goal of the game is to pat each knee in consecutive order, moving around the circle. Once again, a few dry runs are required to work out the kinks. As the competition begins, if a player pats out of order, she must remove the offending hand and place it behind her back. That knee is then skipped in the order. As the game proceeds, players must skip over other players with both hands behind their backs and maintain the order of the circle. The class should practice going in both directions. As players master the game, a variation is added. If a player pats twice on a knee, the direction is reversed and the pats proceed in the opposite direction. The game continues until there are too few hands left to continue. It is a deceptively simple game yet proves amusingly difficult. Again, it teaches observation and concentration and helps to break down physical barriers in the group.

## One Word at a Time Story

This is a game devised by Keith Johnstone, whose work will form the basis for the class's first platform.[1] It is good to do it after Pat, so that the class is still sitting and is, perhaps, less self-conscious. The point is to construct a story collectively, a single word at a time, while moving around the circle. Students are made aware of what kills a story: violation of rudimentary grammar, violations of logic (allowing, of course, for a certain latitude in terms of absurdity), overlong pausing, and needless repetition. What builds a story is referring back to established elements and creating a specific circle of logic within which the story takes place. It is a good idea to request suggestions from the class in terms of genre, such as science fiction, romance, horror, or fairy tale. The first go-round is usually pretty rocky. The instructor can help students by advising them to look the next player in the eyes and give him just the word he needs to keep the story going, instead of focusing on getting the "correct" word. This suggestion usually improves the results markedly, and quite a few interesting though rather abstruse stories can be generated. With increased speed comes a lessening of the need to get it right. The benefits are diffusing of self-consciousness through the shared responsibility of storytelling and an understanding of the imperative of forward motion and adaptability in telling a story.

## The Story Assignment

The first assignment for the class is the story assignment. For this exercise, the actors are invited to bring in a section of text to read in front of the class. It can be as brief as a couple of sentences and should be no longer than three to four minutes. It can be a simple quote, a journal entry, a song lyric, or a section from a book or magazine. One student I had even brought in a magazine ad for a sports car. What is most important is that each person chooses the text because it holds a specific meaning for him or her. It can be humorous, painful, or inspiring. It can also be mundane. The only parameter is that whatever is shared has meaning for the student.

A chair is placed in front of the class. When an actor voluntarily takes the chair, he is greeted by enthusiastic applause. He shares his text without explanation or introduction. When he is finished, he receives another round of enthusiastic applause. When the last student has shared her text, the group convenes in a circle to discuss the experience.

This is a crucial element of the exercise. For one thing, everyone has the opportunity to assess whatever obstacles he or she encountered in sharing—such as specific tensions, nervousness, or shyness. It's good to ask questions of the group. Did they focus on the text or on the audience with whom they were sharing? What changed physically when they took the chair? Did they feel vulnerable? Everyone also has the opportunity to express what he or she experienced as audience members.

Typically, the process is revelatory. There is certain to be a great variance in the degree of risk and vulnerability each student assumes in sharing with the class. But even the briefest or seemingly most benign text is revealing because the actor chose it for its implied meaning; it therefore represents an act of courage. Students are shown facets of one another of which they were previously unaware. This also points out the assumptions we make unconsciously about each other. The exercise further serves the goal of breaking down the distance between students. But most importantly, it reinforces one of the crucial elements of storytelling in general—that the role of the actor is to share meaning with an audience. With the element of choice, this potential is easily accessible. The chore as the class progresses is to find meaning in divergent texts and scenarios and to further explore the means of sharing.

## THE WARM-UP

There are many variations of warm-ups available to actors. As students become more practiced, the warm-up may eventually be personalized and shaped to their own needs. A warm-up should address four related areas: the body, the breath, the voice, and the speech articulators. The purpose of the warm-up is twofold: first, to extend the range of expressivity before performing and second, to assess the state of the actor's instrument on a given day.

In baseball, a pitcher warms up in the bullpen not merely to prepare his body for his upcoming task, but also to monitor which of his pitches are working for him. In his array of tools, he must discern which he feels most confident in before he relies on it in a pressure situation. It is much the same for an actor when she performs.

The warm-up I describe is an amalgamation of many different sources, including much longer and more specific warm-ups designed by noted teachers such as Kristen Linklater and Edith Skinner.[2] In the interest of efficiency, I have structured the warm-up to take less than fifteen minutes.

## *Body*

I start with the class standing in a circle a few feet from each other with their feet roughly shoulder-width apart. First, I invite the students to become aware of everything that is going on with them in their lives and to try to become conscious of how this is affecting them physically. I then ask them to respond to that knowledge by stretching or moving their bodies in whatever way they need in that moment. I encourage them to yawn and allow themselves to vocalize any sounds they feel their bodies require.

After a few moments, I direct them to shake out one hand, then the other, one foot, and then the other. I ask them to clasp their hands together into a fist, hold it in front of them, and give it a vigorous shake, loosening their whole bodies. Next, I ask students to imagine a ladder dangling in front of them. I ask them to climb the imaginary ladder by reaching up with one hand and grabbing a rung, then reaching up with the other hand, and so on, alternating hands.

I then ask them to stretch up their arms and extend their fingers and imagine that they are dangling from strings connected to each finger controlled by a puppeteer. The puppeteer then cuts the strings to the fingers and their hands drop down to the wrists, which are controlled by two different strings. These strings are then cut, and the arms collapse to the elbows, which have their own set of strings. The strings to the elbows are in turn cut, and the arms collapse to the sides.

Next, the head drops forward, and I ask students to give in to the weight of their heads and gradually fold down vertebra by vertebra until they are hanging forward from their hip sockets with their knees slightly bent. I now ask them to take a deep breath and let the exhalation fall to the floor on an *f* sound. Students then gently nod their head "yes" in this upside down position, and then gently shake their head "no." The next step is to bend the knees a little more and tuck the tailbone under and gently stack the vertebrae one on top of the other to a standing position, letting the neck and head float up last.

As the students next inhale, they float their shoulders up toward their ears. They are invited to experience the new body position of tensed shoulders before they release them. As the breath is released, the shoulders drop to a relaxed position. This is repeated three times, with the students first dropping the shoulders exaggeratedly forward and then backward and finally toward the center, each time noting the psychological state that each shoulder position suggests. The dropped forward position is a classic submissive indicator, and the expansive backward drop is an indicator of dominant behavior.

I then ask students to let their heads drop forward and slowly circle them around to the right, being especially aware of the channel running through the center of the body that is created as the head rolls back. After two or three times around, they change direction. When they have explored both directions. They reverse direction again, this time allowing the shoulders to follow and give in slightly to the weight of the head and neck. After another change of direction, students let the knees and hips enter into the equation, forming a counterpoint to the head and shoulders so that the whole body is wiggling like a wet noodle.

## Breath

Next, students focus on their breath. Placing a hand lightly on their abdomens just below the belly button, students stand in a relaxed position. I then invite them to feed in the impulse for a pleasurable sigh of relief from wherever they are in their day, their week, and with whatever is going on presently in their lives. They then release the sigh on breath alone. After three sighs, each one fed by the impulse for a pleasurable sigh of relief, I invite the students to feed in more energy. They now pant in and out on breath before releasing into the sigh. This is repeated twice. The next step is for students to vacuum out their lungs. This process, devised by Kristin Linklater, is important for increasing capacity and for sensitizing students to the value of diaphragmic breathing. The students gradually exhale, during which they bend the knees and gently shake the body. When all the breath is spent, students pinch their nostrils closed and wriggle up through the torso as they assume a full standing position. When they reach their full height, they release the nostrils, allowing the air to come rushing in and fill the lungs. They then resume their normal breathing before repeating the process twice more. This should be done slowly as the repeated loss and sudden return of oxygen can make one light-headed.

## Voice

Students now move on to the voice. Again, encourage them to sigh with relief, this time releasing it on a vocalized *aaah*. This is repeated three times, followed by two repetitions of a vocalized pant. It is crucial that the impulse for a pleasurable sigh of relief underlies all the voice production in the warm-up.

Students now explore their vocal range and resonators. Standing up straight, students drop their heads backward, creating an open channel to their diaphragms. In this position, students are instructed to release the sigh on a velvety blue *aaah* sound, gently patting their upper chests with a hand as they paint the ceiling with their voices. After two such exhalations, students bring the head back on the spine and exhale on an *eh* sound, while using their hands to rub their faces, loosening the skin. After two long exhales, the head drops slightly forward, and students sigh out on a very nasal *mee* sound. As they sigh, students use the first two fingers of each hand to massage both sides of the nose. Again, after two repetitions, students are asked to place the flat of one palm on the very crown of the skull. They are invited to feel the vibrations in the hand as they explore the very highest part of the range on a *mee-eee-eey-eee* sound.

After another two exhalations, have students bend their knees and slowly circle their hips as they explore the bottom of their range. As they exhale on an *oh* sound, they are to imagine stirring a thick, bubbling vat of molasses. After repeating two times, the class comes to a comfortable standing position. After another invitation to sigh with relief, they move through their range, going from the *oh* to the *aaah* to the *eeh* to the *mee*, all the way to the highest *mee-eee-eey-eee*. Now starting from the highest point, they reverse the process and go back down the range as they drop down through their spines. Students hang in this position, with arms and head dropped toward the floor. After a moment, they inhale and move from the low *oh* back up through all the resonators as they build back up the spine one vertebra at a time.

Finally, from a standing position, they are asked to produce a huge sigh of relief and release through all the resonators on the way down and then again on the way up as they come back to standing all on a single breath. After this process, they are asked to breathe normally and repeat some sighed sounds such as *hummm, hummuh, hee-yah, hee-ya-ya,* and *hummuh-ya-ya-la-la-la.*

## Speech Articulators

The class is now ready to approach the last part of the warm-up, the speech articulators. I ask the students to rub their hands vigorously together to create friction, and then use their hands to loosen up the skin on the face. They are then asked to put their pinky fingers in both corners of their mouths and stretch out their lips and mouths. Next, they sigh out through closed lips so that the lips flutter with the vibrations. They are then asked to use the muscles in the face to make their faces as large and open as possible. They alternate this with scrunching up the face and making it very small and tight. This is done three times. Next, the class is asked to chew with their entire faces and alternate with chewing vigorously with their mouths only. I then ask them to smile with their entire faces and to alternate with smiling with only their mouths. The latter tends to look like high school yearbook photos.

After this, students rub the heels of their hands together and put them on either side of their faces where the jaw meets the skull. Then, they are asked to very gently, using gravity, allow the hands to take any tension from the jaw and move it down through the face until it falls onto the floor. This process is repeated three times. Next, with the thumb and forefinger of each hand, students take hold of their chins. The jaw drops and students use their hands to bring the lower teeth back up to meet the upper teeth. After doing this three times, students, while concentrating on the cool air rushing in and out over the very back of their tongues as they breathe, give their jaws a vigorous but gentle shiver. It is of the utmost importance that no one over exerts himself muscularly, as the goal is freedom and relaxation.

Students then touch the very tip of their tongue with their pinky rather forcefully in order to activate and sensitize it. They then touch the tip of the tongue to the top lip, bottom, left, and right in varying order and follow by circling the tip of the tongue around the lips to the right and then again to the left. The tongue is then placed behind the lower teeth and students are asked to arch the middle of the tongue forward and then relax it. It helps at this point to have them place a hand on the chin to make sure the jaw doesn't jut forward as the tongue arches. Next, students, while concentrating on the cool air rushing in and out over the back of the tongue and with its tip still touching the lower teeth, give the middle of the tongue a wiggle like a wet rag. This can be a little difficult for some students, and it should be stressed that dexterity comes with practice.

Finally, the students breathe in and out on a *kuh* sound while stretching their bodies in a catlike way. They are now ready to drill the articulators. It helps for the instructor to have a sense of the optimal sounds produced, as the goal is precision and clarity. Students begin by making a popping sound with their lips. Then they drill.

The following consonant and vowel sounds are to be repeated by the class en masse:

puh, puh, puh—buh, buh, buh
tih, tih, tah—dih, dih, dah
kih, kih, kah—gih, gih, gah

This series is to be repeated rapidly and then reversed.

Students then pronounce "paper poppy" followed by "baby bubble," alternating the phrases and repeating each three times. The next series is "lilly, lolly, looly, lawly," again repeated at least three times rapidly. This is followed by "wee, wah" then "eee, you, ah, ooh," each repeated three times rapidly.

The next series is toned consonants:

ma, may, me, my, mo, moo
na, nay, ne, ny, no, noo
nga, ngay, nge, ngeye, ngo, ngoo
ahm, aim, eem, I'm, ohm, oom
on, ain, een, I'n, own, oon
ong, aing, eeng, I'ng, owng, oong

Next are toned endings, each repeated rapidly three times:

Close, Clothe, Clove
Closed, Clothed, Cloved
Close, Clothes, Cloves

The following should be repeated very quickly without the consonants bleeding into one another:

Did you? Would you? Could you?
Can't you? Won't you? Don't you?
Didn't you? Wouldn't you? Couldn't you?
Ralph Roister Doister
Sister, wishes, vicious, judicious, whispers, fishes, mister,
    masters, seizures, fissures

It is now a good time to introduce a tongue twister. Any challenging one will do. I use this:

Betty Botta bought some butter. But, said she this butter's
bitter. If I put it in my batter, it will make the batter bitter.
But a bit of better butter will make the bitter batter better. So
t'was better Betty Botta bought a bit of better butter.

After they have completed the drills, I have them repeat the following in various pitches and using different resonators and intentions:

Why? No? OK! Huh? No way! Oh no. Yeah, right. Me? You!
    Come here. Go away!

I finish the warm-up by having them repeat an excerpt from the "The Walrus and the Carpenter" by Lewis Carroll,[3] line by line, starting in a whisper and then growing in vocal strength and volume:

The time has come the walrus said to talk of many things
of shoes and ships and ceiling wax
of cabbages and kings
and why the sea is boiling hot
and whether pigs have wings

Thus ends the warm-up. It may take longer than fifteen minutes at first, as students get familiar with it. It needn't be done every class as it will take away class time that needs to be spent on a range of exercises. However, it should be returned to with some frequency so that any of the actors will be able to successfully lead it by the end of the semester.

# PLATFORM 1: IMPROVISATION, KEITH JOHNSTONE

The following sections are allotted to theories and exercises that offer students a range of tools to use as they move toward interpreting texts. The first platform is improvisation. Other than monologues and auditions, there is virtually no other aspect of acting that can intimidate an actor more than the thought of improvising in front of a live audience. The reason for this is simple: Improvisation is greatly perceived as a vehicle for only the cleverest, quickest, and most thick-skinned members of the profession. Improvisation audiences are seen as a hungry mass that thrive on the discomfort of the performers and expect a constant buffet of laugh lines. The reason to confront the challenge of improvising early on is to quell these assumptions and explore the true possibilities of improvised theatre and how it can reveal broader truths about acting and storytelling in general.

There is a long tradition of improvisation, from its earliest roots in commedia dell'arte through the groundbreaking work of innovators such as Viola Spolin and Del Close. I have been exposed to many different techniques and approaches to improvisation, but the approach that I personally find most relevant toward acting in general and, more specifically, to storytelling is the work of Keith Johnstone. Johnstone has written two seminal books that I heartily recommend: *Impro* and, appropriately enough, *Impro for Storytellers*. He has trained actors at the Royal Academy of Dramatic Art and the Royal Court Theatre, has led workshops across Canada, the United States, and England, and is the founder of the International TheatreSports.[4]

He devised his techniques, as many great teachers do, in response to the deficiencies he saw in his own teachers, some of whom he found to be too result oriented and whose teaching failed to produce either spontaneity or humanity in students. In class, Johnstone cites the W. B. Yeats quote: "Education is not filling a bucket, but lighting a fire." Indeed, there is something entirely liberating about Johnstone's teaching and approach and what it affords the actor. Johnstone took as his inspiration the English pro-wrestling bouts that were performed as a kind of working-class spectacle in public cinemas. He was amazed at the enthusiasm of the audience and wondered if such excited and invested responses could replace the typical culturally accepted behavior of audiences in mainstream theatre. This led him to devise the controlled anarchy of TheatreSports. In this format, two teams face off in a series of game challenges that are overseen and arbitrated by a panel of "judges," which feature outrageous penalties and rewards for the players. This context creates a spirit of fun and chaos that pervades both the playing and the watching. While it is difficult in the context of an acting class to establish all the ground rules of the TheatreSports model, we can look to Johnstone's words and advice and to a selection of the games themselves to give us an entrée into the world of improvisation.

> Improvisation is not a normal situation. Most of the improvisation one sees is drowning people pulling each other under. It devolves into a battle for control. That is because we all have a universal fear of being looked at. Much of what we think of as improvisation is people giving in to their fear and their desperation to stay in control. Fear makes actors not relate to each other, which is the opposite of what the audience comes to see. Audiences come to see something happen, not to see people being clever. It is non-intellectual. Good scenes are not primarily verbal. They are about changing relationships between people. . . . As an actor, you are not there to tell jokes. You are there to expose yourself.
>
> "People are protective in life, which is detrimental to impro," as Johnstone calls it. "Actors give in to the need to control or avoid circumstances that could alter them. The stage needs to be an area where you enter states of danger, hoping to survive, but not

caring if you don't. In the end, the audience wants somebody in trouble. Children play games to experience risk. They find risk pleasurable. But it changes as we age. We get safer. Safety, however, is not pleasurable. If you can't fail, it turns into work. Children naturally go forward. Adults, however, tend toward inertia. Inertia is just one of many defense mechanisms. Most improv actors don't stay in the present tense. They drift off into the "what I did" or "what I'm planning to do." They tamp down their enthusiasm in order to lessen the fall of failure.

Yet, even when an actor "fails," if he responds good-naturedly, the audience will warm to him. This is the opposite of life, where if we play the penitent and beat ourselves up, the less other people will punish us. That doesn't work onstage. In Impro we look for good nature amidst failure. In Impro, the harder you try, the worse it is.[5]

But when improvisers know what they should do, they don't do it. The body knows what to do, but actors let their minds give in to the obligation to be "clever" and "original." That is why Johnstone advises actors to "be boring" and "be obvious." "To get past the fear," he says, "try to be average, don't try to be your best. . . . You don't have to be better than you are." When an actor goes onstage to be funny, he is surrendering all his power. In contrast to the actors' expectations, the audience actually wants what we consider "obvious." Every time a situation is established, it contains a circle of expectations. A pirate ship may entail parrots, prostheses, and treasure. A desert implies sand, mirages, and romantic sheiks. Yet if an improviser introduces an absurd juxtaposition such as an ice-cream vendor in order to be original, he may get a laugh, but he will kill the chances of the audience engaging in the story. The key is to stay in the circle, not demolish it.

Similarly, actors are terrified of the "nothing." This forces them into manic states of activity in which they reach for whatever they think the audience will find funny or absurd. Yet there has to be a "nothing" for "something" to emerge. It is part of the process. If the actors stay calm and positive and are trying to inspire one another, a relationship emerges. Once the situation is clear and the scene finds its balance, the improvisers introduce a "tilt" that upsets the stability. This is the primary structure for impro as well as for most drama in general.

You may recognize that what Johnstone found through his direct experience is very similar to what Aristotle found in his analysis of drama in *Poetics*. As Johnstone notes, we pay money to watch people being altered. The "change" that Aristotle describes is the "tilt" advocated by Johnstone. The players establish a relationship, and then create a tension, which the tilt shifts. The key is to create stabilities and then upset them.

For example, a scene begins between a man and woman in a restaurant. As it proceeds, we come to realize that they have been seeing each other for a while and they are both eager for the relationship to move forward. He then introduces a tilt by saying he wants her to meet his mother and she is at the restaurant. When the third player enters, she assumes the role of a feral dog. The man then explains that he was raised by wolves. While the idea of this tilt is funny, what makes the scene work is the new tensions it provides. He is hoping his girlfriend won't react badly to this news and wants his mother to behave. The girl loves him and is trying not to be too put out by a very strange situation. Meanwhile, the mother has the splendid tension of being a wild dog in a restaurant with her adopted son and his potential fiancé. This new platform allows for many playable possibilities. What makes situations like this pleasurable for the audience is the struggle of the characters to maintain their dignity and a sense of normalcy even in extraordinary situations. This tension is the bread and butter for an impro actor. It's all about struggling within extreme circumstances. All great scenes need this imbalance. Once a tilt happens, a new stability will set in that will require a new tilt. It can be any idea that changes the relationship.

So before we get to the games let us summarize some helpful guidelines:[6]

- Stay positive. Accept any ideas from your partner(s) as a gift.
- Don't try to control a scene. A corollary is "Make blind offers, not controlling offers." The difference is saying "I've got you a present! Go on open it!" as opposed to "I've got you a present! It's a python!" The first, blind offer allows the player

to respond and participate in the creation of the situation. The controlling offer demands that the second player accept the choice forced upon him.

- Walk onstage to inspire your partner. Value your idea by its effect on the other person.
- Do only scenes that you want to do. Often times, scenes suggested by the audience are designed to humiliate the players. So don't do those scenes. Have a good time onstage. If you can maintain the pleasure in any task, you will get better.
- Stay calm. If you have nothing, the audience will watch if you're calm. Don't give signals of physical tension. Great entertainers make people relax.
- Don't plan ahead. Don't dwell on what just happened. Stay in the now.
- Dare to be boring. Don't be original. Don't be clever. Don't do your best.
- Create specific circles with your partner. The more specific, the better.
- After you've created the circle and the stability sets in, find the tilt. It is any idea that allows for change.
- Be obvious. Give the audience what they want. The goal is not to impress them with how clever or funny you can be, but rather to turn them into one large animal, anticipating and responding as one.

## THE GAMES

Although the games exist in no particular order, I've tried to list them in a way that might suggest a progression. I've also listed some of the challenges and focuses of the games. Bear in mind, these are only the opinions of the author. I will mention what Johnstone himself says of the games. He says they are based on the following ideas:[7]

- That improvisers defend themselves against imaginary dangers as if these dangers were real.
- That "splitting the attention" allows some more creative part of the personality to operate.

- That drama is about dominance and submission.
- That stories achieve structure by referring back to earlier events.
- That the spectators want to see the actors in states of transition, and being altered by each other.
- That improvisers need "permission" to explore extreme states.
- That when we think ahead, we miss most of what's happening onstage (as in life).

## The Hat Game

As the name implies, this game involves hats, two in fact.[8] The best are soft felt hats with a decent crown and not too wide a brim. Baseball hats can be used in a pinch, but they can be problematic as they increase the risk of fingers in faces. Two players each wear a hat while they sit next to each other on a sofa. (They can also sit in chairs facing each other in a pinch.) They are instructed to engage each other in conversation. In terms of subject matter, it is usually best to stay within the parameters of their common experience at first. During the conversation, they each are to try and take the hat cleanly from the other person's head. If successful, they win the game. If they try and fail, they lose. A hat that is merely knocked off represents a failed attempt. The key is to wait until the person is not present. It's an exercise in zen. Each actor should first practice so that he or she is aware of the dangers of roughly thrusting a hand toward a partner's face. Once the game has been played a couple of times (with a champion remaining seated), scenarios can be introduced, such as "You are two monks at a monastery" or "You are both patients at a hair restoration clinic," and conversation must progress accordingly. Speed and agility are not determining factors. Often a hat is taken in what seems like slow motion. If the game slows down, the teacher may say, "If no attempt is made in the next thirty seconds, you both lose." Once they get the hang of it, students may also be liberated from sitting and move about in a more natural scene. Generally, it is a very fun game for both players and audience, as the tension is exquisite. It is a wonderful game to reinforce the importance of staying in the here and now as those who strategize too much tend to be the first ones left hatless.

## Group Yes!

This is a wonderful group game to play early on.[9] It is simple. It is based on the premise that there is no leader and every one acts in service to the group. Any player can suggest simple physical actions such as "let's dance," "let's lie down," or "let's hum *Amazing Grace.*" Every suggestion made by an individual is met with a loud and enthusiastic "Yes!" from the entire group, who then proceed to employ the suggestion. However, players are required to drop out at any point at which they feel reluctant. At first, some players may feel the need to assert their cleverness on the group, but as the players reject jokey or intentionally humiliating suggestions by dropping out, it will tend to reinforce the need for inspiring others rather than gratifying one's own ego. An excellent variation in a large class is to have two "Yes!" groups and allow players to jump to the other group when they feel reluctant. Once a group achieves an overwhelming majority, they are declared the winners.

## What Comes Next?

An element that Johnstone emphasizes is the need to inspire your partner.[10] This serves a dual purpose. It automatically places an actor's attention outside himself, which goes a long way toward eliminating self-consciousness, and it ensures that something will happen, which makes the scene watchable. This game also teaches players how to build a forward-moving narrative and not get caught in the traps of inertia, joking, and negative choices. The game forces actors to inspire their partners.

Five or six players are needed for this game. One player stands while the others sit on a bench. One at a time, players from the bench approach the standing player, who asks, "What comes next?" The player from the bench attempts to construct a narrative that is interesting to the first player, as in "We go for a drink in a seedy bar in Paris." If the first player is indeed inspired by the suggestion, she says OK, and the two actors mime the action. After the action is established, the first player again, "What comes next?," and another suggestion is offered that moves the narrative forward, such as "An old lover of yours is seated nearby." If, however, the first player finds a suggestion uninspiring or simply generic, such as "You win the lottery," then she is free to say no, and the next player from the bench tries his hand at inspiration. Players should alternate being the one inspired and frequently change the narrative.

## What Are You Doing?

This is another good early warm-up game.[11] Two players take the stage. The first player mimes a physical activity. Once it is established, the second player asks, "What are you doing?" The first player responds by naming an activity that he is clearly not doing. For example, a player who is miming an invisible game of tennis could say, "I'm mowing the lawn." At this point the second player performs the activity named by the first player. Once the second player is clearly mowing an invisible lawn, the first player stops his activity, watches the second player, and asks, "What are you doing?" The second player responds by naming another completely unrelated activity, which the first player then mimes, and so on. It is a game that can go on quite awhile and still be enjoyable, but depending on the class size, it is usually best to have about ten switches. It is a great game to propel students into doing rather than thinking and planning.

## Story Off

This is another good early game as it draws on the class's experience with the One Word at a Time Story.[12] Three to five players stand in a row with an additional player, the conductor, seated about five feet away facing them. The conductor, using one of his hands, points to a player who commences a story. While the first player is in the midst of her story, the conductor uses his other hand to point to another player who must seamlessly pick up the story and continue it. This continues until a player commits a violation, at which point the teacher mimes shooting the violator who then replaces the conductor in the chair. Violations are overlong pauses, abhorrent grammar, blatant lapses in logic, or needless repetition. The conductor may also be executed if he goes too quickly or doesn't use both hands in an attempt to trick the other players. The conductor is then replaced from someone in the audience. Once they get the hang of it, the unfolding story can be acted out by other members of the group. The process continues until one storyteller is left. Each time a violation occurs, a new story with a new genre is initiated. If there are separate groups, the reigning champions then compete against each other. This game is a great vehicle to teach listening and the importance of staying in the moment. Students will find that they must think too fast to be able to give in to self-consciousness.

## Status Party

Another crucial element in Johnstone's work is status.[13] Status informs our behavior every day, but for the most part it is unconscious. Every tick or movement we perform or witness in our daily lives acts as a signifier of the desire to either dominate or submit, and yet we are for the most part unaware of them. This game explores these manifestations on a conscious level. Eight to ten players are needed for this game. The players are divided in half into group A and group B. The teacher suggests an environment that requires group interaction, such as a college mixer or a high school reunion. Group A members must make continuous eye contact, keep their heads still, keep their toes turned outward, pause before responding to questions, and use long and complete sentences. Group B members are told to make eye contact only intermittently, respond immediately, speak in fragments, and get out of breath. They touch their own heads and faces and turn their toes inward. Everyone is told to concentrate only on the physical adjustments. As they make conversation and the scene proceeds, it is fascinating to see the status roles and characters that emerge in a kind of collaboration between the performers and those observing. The game emphasizes both the dynamics of status in scene work and the power of simple physical adjustments in determining character.

## Status Party with Cards

Six or seven players work well for this version.[14] Again, choose an environment that requires interaction, such as a fancy ball, a wedding reception, or a convention. From a deck of cards, each player draws a card. Players must not look at the cards. They hold the cards face out against their foreheads so that others can see the card but they cannot. The cards denote status, ace being the highest and two the lowest. Explain to the players that those with high-status cards (ace, king, queen) are the most desirable and popular, whereas those with low-status cards (two, three, four) are the least desirable. The scene commences, and players interact based on how they perceive the status of the others. These interactions then inform the players of their own status. After a few minutes, end the game and ask the players to form a line in the order of status as they perceive it to be. It is very rare for the group not to get the exact order of status. It is a wonderful game to inform about the power of perception and projection of status.

A variation of the game has the cards dealt but seen only by the players who receive them. The cards are not held to the forehead, and only the behavior of each player determines his or her status.

## Status Party with Endowment Cards

This is my own adaptation of the previous game, and it is a great means of asserting the feedback loop that governs our behavior. Each player is handed a card and again places it on his or her forehead facing outward so that the player cannot read it. In lieu of numbers, the following attributes are written on the cards: drunk, sexy, injured, foreign, dumb, rich, annoying, insecure, rude, lecherous, cool, racist, famous, smelly, and beautiful. There are a host of other attributes the instructor can come up with depending on the size of the class. The entire class should then participate in an improvised cocktail party. The key to the game is for the players to be somewhat discreet in their reactions. Each player's goal is to have a good time, and that will naturally govern whom he or she gravitates toward and how each will react. It is immensely enjoyable as each player starts receiving signals and innately takes on the projected characteristics. Afterward, each player stands in a circle with the cards still in place and tries to guess his or her own endowment.

## High / Low Status

This game is a good follow-up to the status party games.[15] It is best to start with a relatively neutral situation. I tend to like a shop with a shopkeeper and a customer. The customer can be shopping for a ring or taking in a watch or a cell phone to be repaired. The scene starts with each player at neutral status, and the interaction inevitably ends up being simply transactional. After a few minutes, end it after a couple of minutes. Then, instruct one of the players to decrease in status and the other to rise. The scene takes on a very different dynamic as a result, for example:

A: Excuse me, uh, Sir? I think I would like to look at those rings?
B: You let me know when you're sure.
A: No, I mean I do want to see them. Can you help me?
B: I am a jeweler not an optometrist.
A: Well, I mean I can see them. But I want you to show them to me.
B: Very well, (*He points.*) they're right there.
A: Well, I know that . . .

The scene proceeds along these lines for a few minutes. It is then halted and the status is reversed. Another example:

A: You there, with the toupee!
B: Er, what can I do for you?
A: You can start by doing your job. I need to buy some jewelry.
B: Well, what did we have in mind today?
A: I haven't the faintest idea what's in your mind. But I want to buy a ring for my fiancée.

B: Well, do you know what she likes?

A: Of course I know what she likes! I just said I'm marrying her, didn't I?

The players can also create variety in the status transaction by alternating raising their partners and lowering themselves, as in "A good-looking guy like you, I bet you get all the girls. My mom doesn't let me have girls over." The player's job is to lower her partner's status by insulting him or through the player's own self-aggrandizement or to raise the partner's status by complimenting him or by the player demeaning herself. After the new status relationships are established, halt the scene again and instruct the players to reverse the status in the course of the scene. There doesn't have to be a logical reason for the flip, as long as both players commit to it. This is a great means to demonstrate the importance of power and status in scene work and also how the shifting of status relationships creates movement in a scene.

## Fight for Your Number

This game employs a simple scenario and forces the players to work to establish their status.[16] Two players sit in a living room. They are roommates and are having a conversation about asking the third roommate to leave. The third player enters, and they have it out. Before the scene starts, each player must pick one of three numbers representing status, one being the highest, two the middle, and three the lowest. During the course of the scene, each player reads the others' choices and fights to get the numbers they have chosen by alternating raising or lowering his or her own status or that of the other players. Afterward, the spectators judge who won which number. It is a great exercise in anchoring the use of status in relationships.

## Making Faces in Threes

This is another status-based game with a dose of antiauthoritarianism thrown in.[17] Three players sit in three chairs placed in a line. The center position is the boss and the chairs to the right and left are workers. I recommend that the teacher take the role of the boss for the first couple of times as the role is a bit tricky; also, undermining the instructor's position of authority adds to the game.

A profession is chosen at random; virtually any job works well. The boss has brought his two workers in to the office for a discussion. He can be pleased or displeased with their work or just want feedback on his company. The catch is that every time he turns to talk to one of the two employees, the other makes an outrageous face at him behind his back. If an employee is caught making a face, the boss fires her and replaces her with another worker. The tricky part for the boss is to sense when to engage the other worker and almost catch her. He can then confront her, for example:

A: Is there something wrong with your face, Smith?
B: I just had some dental work at lunch and the anesthetic is wearing off.
A: Good for you, doing that on your own time. (*He turns to worker C.*) Jones, why are you smiling?
C: I'm just so very pleased to be spending time with you, Sir!

The boss plays high status, and the employees alternately lower his status (by mocking him behind his back) and raise it (when covering up to his face). The obliviousness of the boss is part of what makes the game fun, so he should not focus on trying to catch the workers making faces. Rather, the boss should focus on his reasons for calling the meeting and only fire a worker when there is a blatant transgression. This is a version of one of Johnstone's master-and-servant games, and it clearly demonstrates the role of status in comedy.

## Questions / Three-Word Scenes / Last Letter / Letter S

The challenge of these four games is for players to stay in the moment, engage with their partner, and not retreat into their own minds.[18] They are competitive one-on-one games. The first game is simple. Every line between the two players must be a question. A player loses when he or she makes a statement or if the instructor decides that the player has introduced a non sequitur or repeated a question, for example:

A: How's it going?
B: Do you really want to know?
A: What's wrong?
B: Do you know Sheila?
A: Do you mean your mistress?
B: How did you know she was my mistress?
A: Did I say mistress?
B: Who told you?
A: Do you know Fred in accounting?
B: Do you mean the fellow with the hairlip?
A: Is that what it's called?

You get the idea. Adept players can go quite a while, and the trick is to keep the logic of the scene going as the questions mount. Similarly, the three-word scene requires that each line have only three words, for example:

A: Hey there, Sally!
B: My old friend!
A: How you been?
B: I can't complain.
A: You look great!
B: Thanks, you too.
A: How is Bob?
B: We got divorced.
A: Never liked him.
B: His secretary did.
A: The lousy dog!
B: I miss him.
A: Sure you do.
B: What about you?
A: Lost my job.
B: Sorry to hear.
A: Yeah, still drinking.
B: You always did!

The more difficult the challenge, the more fun it is to watch. As Johnstone says, it is interesting when people don't know what to say. Often, the difficulty is read as emotion, and if the actor remains calm, he will seem to be wrestling with his internal state. Early on, it's advisable to count contractions, such as *I'm, won't, isn't, aren't,* as single words in order not to completely paralyze the players. Later, as players get up to speed, contractions can be banned. It is interesting how the games, if played fast and without pauses, start to sound like contemporary dialogue like something out of the work of David Mamet or Harold Pinter.

Last Letter is a good progression from the two previous games as it requires players to think and do simultaneously. The rule is simple: Every line spoken by one of the players has to begin with the last letter of the previous line, for example:

A: How are you?
B: Unfortunately, not well.
A: Larry, you're kidding, right?
B: Truth be told, I could go at any moment.
A: Terrible news. No hope then?
B: None whatsoever.
A: Rough going. Well, it's been a pleasure knowing you.
B: Usually, I would agree. But seeing as I don't have long to live I'm trying to be more truthful. I never cared for you.
A: Up yours then!
B: No need to get vulgar.
A: Rot in hell!

A variation is to have the actors play a scene without using the letter *s*. Another is to alternate letters through the alphabet. The game is successful if players continue to play action and attempt to affect the other players, as opposed to merely trying to survive.

## Stand, Sit, Lie Down / Two Up, One Down / Four Chairs

The exercises tend to stretch out over days and when starting a new day, the energy and focus of the class may need to be reestablished.[19] These games are a good means for getting players physically and mentally aware for the more complex games. The ground rules are simple. In Stand, Sit, Lie Down, three players occupy the space with the only rule being that one must be seated, one lying down, and one standing. When one player alters their position, each must adjust accordingly. At first, the changes are tentative, and the instructor may ask them to increase the tempo. After they have got the hang of it, they can play a simple scene with words, such as waiting for a bathroom or getting ready for a party. This game should not be allowed to go too long as it serves as a setup for the next two.

In Two Up, One Down, the title is pretty explanatory. Three players take the space and one stays on the ground while the other two stand. They then change positions and adjust as in the first game. They will master this quickly. When they do, two more players are added, and the game becomes Three Up, Two Down. Just when they are on the point of mastering this, two more players are added, and the game becomes Four Up, Three Down. At this point, the game becomes fun to watch. As more players are added, the tempo naturally increases as the ability to count quickly diminishes. The game becomes enjoyable for the audience because of the embarrassed adjustments the players make as they quickly try to keep track of the count.

After this has progressed, the time is right for Four Chairs. Four chairs are set a few feet apart, and players are given four poses: seated with hands on knees, seated with arms folded and legs crossed, standing with arms folded, and standing with hands on hips looking forward. Again, play begins and players are allowed to switch poses while consciously looking at one another. After a few rounds of switches, players are informed they must use only their peripheral vision. The viewers will notice that a bizarre kinetic relationship forms between the players, suggesting a story or subtext surrounding the movements. All these games form a foundation for the ensuing games.

## Speak in One Voice

One of Johnstone's discoveries is that we all have an innate ability to communicate verbally simultaneously.[20] This is akin to the group consciousness arrived at in Group Yes! The process begins by the instructor having the class say simple phrases such as "good morning" along with the instructor without knowing what's coming next. This forces anticipation and adaptation. Next, the instructor establishes a simple dialogue with the entire class, having them answer en masse as one character. This requires a rather slow pace and sometimes an answer isn't intelligible. In that case, the instructor asks, "What?," and the class tries to make the answer clearer. It is best at this point to ask relatively simple questions, such as "How old are you," "Where do you live?," and "Do you have a pet?" Having a large number actually makes it easier because it forces the "clever" players into consensus with the group. Once they have gotten through the rocky part, take a large group of men (at least five) and the same number of women and have them play a scene together as two characters. The premise should be simple, such as a boy and girl meet in the park, have a conversation, and agree to go out on a date. Again, if an answer is unintelligible, the other player(s) simply say "What?" Even the simplest scene becomes very enjoyable to watch.

Finally, the instructor integrates the one-voice character into a more challenging scene. I use one scenario where a college student is bringing her new boyfriend home to meet her mother or father. The boyfriend is played by two or more players. They link arms and perform all actions and dialogue simultaneously. It is a good scenario because it forces the boyfriend to respond to the father or mother's interrogation and has a built-in tension to it. Another scenario has three players linked as a husband coming home at 2 a.m. to find his angry wife waiting for him. It's fun in this scene to mix the genders of the husband, such as two men and a woman or two women and a man. This scene is interesting because the husband almost automatically seems guilty because of the hesitancy of the responses. All the one-voice exercises are great for getting players out of their heads and making them simply talk and listen and stay in the moment. It also illustrates the pleasure of being obvious.

## Lip Sync

If the class has mastered Speak in One Voice, this should be a breeze.[21] There are many variations, but I like to use a simple version. In this one, a man and a woman are chosen to play a scene from a foreign movie, which has been dubbed into English. Two other players are selected to be the voices for each respective actor. The audience supplies a genre, such as period romance, spy film, or gangster film. The first two players move their lips and perform the actions suggested by the second pair of players. This requires the second pair to play the scene even though they are not doing it physically. It is imperative to stay simple and obvious and not try to be clever. They also need to adjust their positions so they can have a clear view of the actor whose dialogue they are dubbing. These scenes can be great fun, but they can also get bogged down, so best to keep it short.

## Arms

In this game, a player puts his arms behind his back and another player, standing behind him, inserts his arms to replace them.[22] I like to use two players with surrogate arms for the game, so it is necessary for the players to turn slightly toward the audience to maintain the illusion. A scene played at a bar or a bus stop or in an elevator automatically provides the necessary full frontal view. Many scenarios are available—a high school dance, a singles bar, a broken elevator. The two characters then interact and use their new arms as naturally as possible. One of the actors may try to initiate movement, but the game works best if it is a collaboration. There is also a temptation to have the arms go wild for the sake of laughs, but the scenes will be far more enjoyable if all the players aspire to natural behavior and try to stay cool handling different props and gesturing while maintaining the integrity of the situation.

## Hand on Knee / Endowments

Hand on Knee is a simple game that allows for very real and interesting reactions.[23] Three chairs are set side by side. Players take a seat and are told that they are strangers on a commuter train. The rule is that whenever the center player talks to the player on his right, he puts his left hand on the thigh of the player on his left. When he then talks to the player on his left, the his removes his left hand and places his right hand on the thigh of the player to his right. When the center player is confronted in anyway about his behavior, he must genuinely lack understanding of what the other two players are describing. The increasing levels of discomfort and the ensuing behavior is what makes the game fun for the audience as long as the players maintain the integrity of the situation.

Endowments uses a similar situation and adds layers of complexity. Three strangers are riding on a train. A and C are sitting and B enters about a minute into the scene. A perceives C to be drunk. C perceives A to be speaking a foreign language. When B enters, A perceives B to be completely naked. C perceives everything B says to be hysterically funny. B perceives both A and C to be young children. It is important that players react to these stimuli spontaneously and truthfully and do not try to broadcast their reactions. If they can, the scene takes on a life of its own and becomes very funny without anyone trying to make it so. Different scenarios can be employed with different endowments.

## Endowment Party

This game is another version of Endowments. In it, one player plays the host and three other players knock on the door and enter as guests.[24] Each player endows each of the other players with the following three following qualities: (1) someone you want to make love to, (2) someone who you perceive as violent and dangerous, and (3) someone who makes you laugh. The catch is that there is no agreement among the players on who is being endowed, so that each player can represent any of the three different endowments to different players. As a result, the party takes on the dynamic of the players' points of view. The game emphasizes the importance of endowments in establishing point of view. It can be played with different endowments or in a specific gibberish, such as Italian or Chinese, for variation.

## Invisible

A similar skill set to Endowments is required for this game.[25] Two players enter a space. It is important for this game, as in most impro games, to have lots of props on hand. You can set up the scene by having two roommates just moving into an old apartment that they got for a cheap rent. The catch is whenever a player leaves, he is invisible when he reenters. This means that whenever that player pulls out a chair, or picks up a book, or handles any prop, that prop is moving by itself in the other player's eyes. Similarly, when the "invisible" player touches the other, that player cannot see what touched her. The game usually starts out slow, but as the strangeness mounts and if the players can maintain their perceived reality, it becomes very enjoyable to watch.

## Emotional Quadrants

This is scene is typically done with two male-female couples, but the numbers and genders can be adjusted.[26] It is good to establish a simple scenario such as a married couple inviting another married couple over for dinner. The playing area needs to be laid out clearly. I usually have a center table with chairs, chairs in each corner of the playing area or "room," and a kitchen counter running along one side. I like to instruct the players away from the audience's hearing because it makes the game more bizarre and therefore more fun to watch. The simple rule is that there are two imaginary lines that cross at the center of the room dividing it into four equal quadrants. When any player enters the first quadrant, he or she is angry. When a player enters the second quadrant, he or she is overwhelmed by sadness. When a player enters the third quadrant, he or she feels very sexy. When a player enters the final quadrant, everything is hysterically funny. Two or more players can inhabit any quadrant at the same time. Again, it is important for the players to maintain the story of the scene and justify the behavior without letting things descend into chaos too early. Almost inevitably, the scene ends up resembling the latter part of Edward Albee's *Who's Afraid of Virginia Woolf?*

## Paper Flicking

This is another game that only works if players invest in the situation.[27] Two players are seated on either side of a desk. B is interviewing A for a job. A needs the job very much, and B is responding favorably to the interview. The catch is that B is writing notes during the interview. Every so often she asks A to write down a contact number on the pad. After A has done so, B tears off the page, crumples it, and throws it at A's head. If A confronts B about the behavior, B is utterly confused. If A becomes insistent, it compromises A's chances of being hired. Similarly, B must remain congenial and professional throughout. It is a great game for establishing moment-to-moment behavior connected to internal need.

## Bore the Audience, Emotional Sounds, and Mantras

As we said earlier, improvisation is not about generating clever laugh lines.[28] This is an exercise in creating subtext and dynamics in a simple scene. This particular scene was made up by Johnstone on the spot and has no particular comic or dramatic storyline. Instructors should feel free to make up similar scenes and situations. This one involves a man and a woman.

He: Nice place.
She: I like it. So, you're a freshman.
He: Yes, ma'am.
She: Care for a whiskey?
He: Sure… I'm going to get an A.
She: If you're good you will.
He: I'm not sure I want to do this.
She: You can't back out now.

Now obviously a relationship is implied, but it is essentially arbitrary. Two actors are assigned and work on the dialogue. After they have run it once for the audience, they are taken to the side and given this simple instruction, "Bore the audience without being bored yourselves."[29] Ironically, this simple adjustment tends to make the actors more interesting and the scene more complex. Why? Because it takes the pressure off the actors to be interesting and to convince us that they are who they are pretending to be and that this is actually happening.

The second adjustment that they are given is to use emotional sounds. Simply, this means that in addition to the dialogue, they make nervous giggles, sighs, hums, or contented mmm's, but these sounds should be discreet enough that they are barely noticeable, if at all, to an audience. Again, to the spectators the scene will seem fuller with a deeper level of connection between the players. Johnstone hypothesizes that the verbal, intellectual component of our brains tends to take the reins from the emotional part when we are in a stressful situation (such as being onstage). By reintroducing the emotional component though these sounds, we get both aspects of ourselves working independently, which makes us seem more present and alive. This is a great adjustment to introduce into any scene where actors aren't listening or are anticipating. It forces them to be in the moment and active even when not speaking.

The final adjustment we give our couple is mantras. Counterintuitively, Johnstone found that if an actor repeats a nursery rhyme, such as "Mary Had a Little Lamb" or "Twinkle, Twinkle Little Star," or a bit of doggerel in his head while playing a scene, he will be more attentive and in the moment. The mantra serves to absorb just enough of the actor's concentration to allow unedited impulses and behavior to start to arise. When that inner mantra is made more loaded, as in "I love you" or "I hate you," the actor is still present but seems to project a different quality. It's a way of consciously manipulating the aura that each of us projects unconsciously. However, it is important not to choose an objective in a Stanislavskian manner, such as "I must seduce you." Instead, a mantra can be chosen in opposition to the apparent reality of the scene. A seduction scene in which "I hate you" is used becomes inherently darker with a higher level of tension.

The actors in this scene are instructed to use either "I love you" or "I hate you." As Johnstone explains, each of these phrases is loaded in a different way. "I love you" increases vulnerability. "I hate you" implies power and control. As a further adjustment, the actors are informed that the mantra can actually interfere with speaking at any point. Fascinatingly enough, Johnstone found that this difficulty in forming words reads as emotion to the audience. It's almost as if the spectators are projecting an internal state onto the actors. Now when we watch the final incarnation of the scene, it seems miles away from the first attempt. It appears to be filled with tensions and interpersonal history and has many layers of meaning. Yet, all the adjustments were purely technical. Like many of Johnstone's exercises, these adjustments serve as a means of short-circuiting the actor's conscious mind out of its instinct to control and plan, so that truthful, immediate behavior can emerge.

There are many more games and exercises available in the writings of Keith Johnstone, and many TheatreSports-affiliated groups offer classes and workshops. Seeing Keith Johnstone teach and lead games in person clarified for me that the games are not merely laugh machines. They are a means to create spontaneous human behavior, which is what an audience truly wants. They also serve the purpose of breaking down barriers and giving students a physical experience of moment-to-moment life onstage. This in turn helps to establish a working ensemble. Even with long-established actors, these exercises can rekindle the pure fun of playing and the joy of spontaneous decision making. They also lay the groundwork for the second platform.

# PLATFORM 2: CONSTANTIN STANISLAVSKI

Constantin Stanislavski spent most of his lifetime formulating and refining his system for training actors. For anyone to claim the ability to distill it to its essential components into a few pages would not be doing it justice. However, the beauty of Stanislavski's work is that it remains vital to this day and features clear elements that dovetail into one another in a very accessible way. Understanding the major elements not only gives us access to the most important system of actor training ever devised, it allows us a platform for understanding all the subsequent adaptations and innovations by those who came after him.

Stanislavski devised his system from the inside.[30] As an actor, he was looking for a means to lessen the impediments of tension and self-consciousness and to increase concentration and communication onstage. His system is both insightful and eminently useable. Stanislavski realized that to conquer the awareness of performing for an audience, the actor needed a stronger pull to his attention. Actors enter the stage with a tremendous amount of energy. They need to know where to invest that energy in a way that will support their efforts as opposed to letting it manifest in fear and tension. Stanislavski understood that in order for actors not to focus on showing, they had to be doing. Every actor onstage needs to find the character's purpose. He called this purpose the *objective*. Now the objective is, simply stated, what the character wants. In every play, in every scene, in every moment, there is something that the character desires. It can be simple or complex, but it is always expressed in the form of a verb.

1. I want my mother to acknowledge me.
2. I want sympathy.
3. I want to make everyone miserable.

These desires are expressed in the form of *actions*. An action is what you do to get what you want. In the case of the listed objectives, some actions might be:

1. catalogue my accomplishments, compliment her, intimidate her physically
2. express pain, detail my sufferings, sob quietly
3. interrupt others, insult them, talk only about myself

Now in any given scene, we may find many different actions that a character plays in service to an objective. Some of them are verbal, some physical. Some are direct, some indirect. When a character's action is either rebuffed or is successful, he or she utilizes *adaptation*. This is simply adjusting the character's behavior based on its effect on the other characters. It is something we all do constantly in life. If an action isn't getting us what we want, we try something else. The reactions of others cause the character to choose new actions, modulate the actions he or she is already using, or if the action is successful, find another objective. Stanislavski calls these adjustments in behavior *beats*. (It is now generally accepted to have been a mistranslation of the word *bits*). These beats represent the shifting dynamic of a scene. By tracking the character's objectives, actions, and the beat changes, we can start to build a score of the character's life, moment by moment, throughout the play.

But we are still missing the big picture. A play is a two- or three-hour section of a character's life. We are trying to build a portrait of the character that convinces the audience that the character existed before the play began and will continue on after the play has ended. The play will most often give us a wealth of details that help us to paint this portrait. All the facts and specific information in the play that describes the character and the world he or she inhabits are called the *given circumstances*. The objectives and actions we choose need to conform to our understanding of the character as gleaned from these given circumstances. But the term is more elastic than simply a system for establishing a character's biography. If the conception of the director dictates that the characters are based on animals or if the production dictates that all the scenes are performed on roller skates, these stipulations form the parameters inside which the actor must do his work. The task is to live truthfully inside even the most extreme circumstances.

To create this portrait, we have to provide details and answer questions that the play doesn't ask. That is where we employ *imagination*. Imagination allows us to step into the character's shoes and see what circumstances and events may have transpired that have led to the objectives and actions the character will employ at the threshold of the play's action. To do this work, Stanislavski advocates the use of the *magic if* or the *what if*. The what if is used to marry the actor's own psychology to the world of the character. For example, the actor could ask himself: What if I grew up in an era of unceasing political and physical warfare? What if I was reviled from earliest days for my physical deformities? What if the only stature I ever achieved in my life was for my viciousness in war, and I now find myself in a time of peace and prosperity?

These particular questions can help the actor step into the worldview of Shakespeare's *Richard III* at the play's start. That in turn can help us to find the character's *superobjective*. The term refers to the drives and desires that encompass what the character will do in the course of the play's action. But it is larger. If the play is a snapshot of moments in a character's life, the superobjective represents the journey that leads us to and from those moments. It is the foundation from which the character draws all the objectives and actions that the varying scenes dictate.

Superobjective is also the term that Stanislavski uses to describe the play as a whole. It can be the creative impulse, theme, or inspiration that led the writer to construct the play and thereby contains its meaning. As such, it forms a story that unites the divergent objectives of all the characters contained within it. It may be encompassed in a simple sentence as, "In a world of hypocrisy, a man fights for an ideal."

These terms give us the architecture of Stanislavski's system. The superobjective of the play gives us the basis that allows us to see each character's superobjective. That in turn allows us to have a platform to explore the objectives of the characters in each scene. The objectives provide the engine for the actions that the characters perform upon one another. As one character's actions meet another character's actions and they both adapt their behavior, the beat changes that ensue provide the moment-to-moment life of the play.

Still, there is the question of emotion. In Stanislavski's system, it is important to use emotion as a means to obtaining objectives and not as an end in itself. However, the question remains, How do you achieve a truthful emotion onstage? Early in his system, Stanislavski was drawn to work of French psychologist Théodule Ribot. Stanislavski realized that emotions were particularly elusive and were not easily responsive to the demands of actors simply because they had established an analytical framework for using them. Ribot had found that past emotional experiences could be evoked indirectly by exploring the physical circumstances and details that surrounded an emotional episode. Richard Boleslavsky, an esteemed teacher of Stanislavski's early methodology, cited an example of an elderly couple who, when experiencing moments of marital friction, were brought back to a state of mutual devotion by a simple plate of sliced cucumbers. The sensory experience of the cucumbers evoked the memory of a perfect day early in their courtship and, along with the memories, the associated feelings. This is also the basis of conditioned responses explored famously by the Russian psychologist, Ivan Pavlov. Stanislavski found that by exploring the details of a previous experience with strong emotional content, an actor could access an analogous emotion to one she needed to fulfill the actions and given circumstances in a play. This process is called *emotional memory* or *affective memory*. Sometimes after utilizing an emotional episode in the context of a scene, the actor would find that the particular memory was losing its effect. At this point, the actor would need to find another memory to produce a similar response.

This concept would come to be one of the most controversial aspects of the system, as it provided a basis for the understanding and sometime misunderstanding of his methods when they were introduced to the West. Stanislavski himself seemed to have moved away from affective memory in his later years in favor of his method of physical actions. He later found that a physical action based on the circumstances of the play did have the capability of evoking an emotional state. Every physical action has a psychological component, and this is the crux of the Method.

For example, if you were to spontaneously pick up a chair and hurl it across the room, you would have both a physiological and an emotional response. Your heart rate would increase, adrenaline would be introduced into your system, and your breathing would intensify. These would be all the signifiers of a violent emotion and you would in fact feel that emotion. It is an extreme example. I have actually demonstrated this in a class, but I don't recommend it unless you have expendable furniture and a fairly durable classroom. The point is that the emotion is inherent to the physical action. I did not need to motivate the action or access a previous memory to perform the action and feel the ensuing emotions. The key is to endow the space and the physical environment so that interactions within it have the capability to feed the situations. For example, a very poor man painstakingly saves a bit of money from his meager paycheck every day for five years to buy his long-suffering wife an anniversary present. The methodical care with which he counts the money will have a distinct emotional component. Conversely, if he goes to the place where he has hidden the money and finds it missing, his search for it will have a tone of panic and despair. If the actor has immersed himself in the given circumstances, these physical actions will release an emotion without his having to resort to any psychological technique. The process by which emotion is inextricably linked to physiology is reinforced by recent research. Dacher Keltner, a professor at Berkeley, has explored the various processes by which emotions are physically manifested and even produced by physical states as indicated by the groundbreaking research of Paul Ekman of the San Francisco State University.[31]

These techniques allow the actor to divide his performance in units. Because he has worked from the superobjective and the given circumstances, he can play these diverse sections with full commitment knowing that they will cohere into a satisfying whole. Together, they form an unbroken line or *through-line* of action that permits the actor to live through each moment of the play.

Stanislavski's work also encompassed the means to create variety in speech and movement and enter into the character and techniques to relax the body and focus the actor's attention. But for our purposes, it is best to tackle the aspects of Stanislavski's system that formed its core foundation. We now have a theoretical understanding of the system, but how do we get it in our bodies?

## HUNTER AND HUNTED

I have seen gifted actors, in trying to play objectives, walk around the stage like pod-people trying to hypnotize their acting partners. It is a common mistake to think that by simply repeating a phrase such as "I must seduce you" over and over in one's mind, an actor is really using an objective. The objective is need. The ways in which that need gets expressed are actions. This is a game that totally immerses the players in objectives and forces them to find physical actions.[32] The object is to win. I make the class repeat this aloud so that it is absolutely clear.

The game requires two blindfolds (bandannas work just fine) and a baton (such as a rolled-up newspaper bound with tape). The class forms two lines facing each other, about twenty-five feet apart. The students sit cross-legged on the floor and close their eyes. The instructor picks two students, one from each line, and secures blindfolds over their eyes as they sit. The instructor then moves to a spot between the two lines and slams the baton to the floor, which signals that the game is to begin. It is a good idea for the instructor to silently move the baton a few feet from the spot where he slammed it because the sound gives a clue to the location.

At this point the students can open their eyes. The two blindfolded players must find the baton, while the others remain seated and watch. Whichever student finds the baton first is the hunter, and the other becomes the hunted. The hunted's objective is to find and sit down in the hunter's vacated spot in the line. The hunter's objective is to touch the hunted with the baton before the hunted can find that spot. If the hunter touches the hunted with the baton, the hunter wins. If the hunted makes it untouched into the hunter's vacated spot, the hunted wins. The rest of the class is not allowed to speak or give clues to the players. However, when the hunted approaches the hunter's spot, they may use their hands to help guide the hunted into position.

The value of the game is that it strips the players of their social defenses and makes them commit completely to the objective. They employ physical actions to find the baton, and both players use a diverse range of strategies once the baton is found. It is very fun to watch, and that is an equally important part of the exercise. The audience learns that the competing actions and objectives create tension, and the release of that tension is what makes watching pleasurable.

## ACTION / OBJECTIVE GLADIATORS

The next exercise forces the players to focus on their partners, who in this game are adversaries. The game is simple. Two students are chosen to play the game. Each student is taken out of the playing space and given an objective. The audience is told what each student's objectives are. The objectives, which are drawn from the bulleted list on the next page, obviously have no connection to any superobjective, and it is hard to imagine a rationale for wanting to achieve most of them. However, these objectives do force the players to strategize and play different actions to attain them. Once a player has achieved his or her objective, the game ends.

After a couple of rounds, players may start to get suspicious of each other and defensive in their behavior, which can slow down the game. If this happens, give the players a minute to achieve their objective and count down every ten seconds. To keep the game going, give players two or even three objectives to try, and the winner is the one who gets any of his or her objectives fulfilled by the other player. The instructor can also keep the game going if one player inadvertently meets the other player's objective, but not as a result of the other player's actions. At first, it is a good idea to have the players be themselves in a neutral situation. After a while, it can become more complex if they are provided with a scenario such as two undertakers preparing a body or a blind date. Listed below are a variety of possible objectives. (Note: Only one objective is used per scene.)

Players try to get their partners to:

- say "I'm sorry," "help," "stop," "please," "what?," or something in a foreign language
- say the name of a food, city, or animal or a color, number, or noun (car, door, chair)
- whistle, hum, scream, make baby sounds, make a kissing sound, whisper, laugh, yawn, or curse
- dance, sing, exercise, jump, or have all four limbs off the floor
- stand on one leg, touch their own face, stick out their tongue, scratch themselves, turn around, sit down, lie down, or run
- touch or hug their partners
- show the other player their butt, teeth, or the sole of their shoe
- throw or hand an object to their partners

While players learn to strategize, they also learn that too much strategizing doesn't help. They have to adapt to their partner. They may have to try and abandon several actions in trying to achieve their objective. The exercise is actually more valuable if they have to work at it and don't get their objective than if they get it right off the bat.

## FAST-FOOD STANISLAVSKI

We return to Johnstone for this exercise that demonstrates both the potential and the pitfalls of the Stanislavski system.[33] It involves some built-in traps, so don't assign this section for reading if you haven't yet done the exercise.

Different scenarios are possible for this game, but we'll use one suggested by Johnstone himself. It is a deathbed scene in which the mother is caring for the infirm father, and the son comes to visit with his new fiancé. That is pretty much all the information you give the players before their first go. The combination of an emotionally loaded scene and the need to play "characters" inevitably leads the actors into playing mood, grasping at clichés, and immersing themselves in stereotypes. This is at best amusing and at worst painful to watch. But it does give us someplace to go.

The next step is to have them all choose an objective to play in the scene and see where it leads them. This second go is inevitably more active but most likely still rather solemn and reverential due to the subject. The choices here generally range from "to prove my love" to " to make peace with my family." The key to breaking the habit of showing rather than doing and reinforcing what the audience already knows is to choose objectives that create dynamic relationships. So Johnstone suggests we have the mother need to get sympathy, the son give everyone a bad time, and the daughter make everyone think she's intelligent. The father tries to cheer everyone up. As Johnstone points out "people don't necessarily change character just because they're ill." So the father and the others aren't limited to the objective of stoically embracing their fate.

After the new objectives have been assigned, the players sit for a few minutes with a pen and paper. Under their assigned objectives they write out lists of actions they can play to get what they want. It is good to encourage speed and lack of consideration in choosing actions. It is simply brainstorming, and there are no bad choices. Some sample actions:

Father
To cheer everyone up (or give people a good time)
- Smile, be friendly
- Compliment others
- Give presents
- Sing show tunes

Mother
To get sympathy from others
- Sigh often
- Have an injury

- Whimper
- Dote on others

Son
To give everyone a bad time (or make everyone miserable)
- Complain
- Interrupt
- Look bored
- Repeat others' words contemptuously

Fiancé
To be intelligent or thoughtful
- Use large words
- Quote others
- Give helpful advice
- Mention books you've read

The lists should be as extensive as possible, but the players shouldn't spend more than about five minutes coming up with them. When they play the scene again, players keep the lists handy so they can refer to them during the scene. Here, the scene finally starts to have life. Players don't feel the obligation to conform to the somber tone of the situation, and they don't fear making a choice that their character wouldn't. They know what to do, and they just have to commit to each action. The cross-purposes create a much more lively and lifelike interaction, and the scene is therefore much more interesting and enjoyable for an audience to watch.

This is but one scenario, and there are many possible objectives that can produce dynamic action lists. Here are a few possible objectives:

- To humiliate someone
- To be thought important
- To fit in
- To seduce someone
- To be thought a jackass
- To confuse someone

If there isn't time to play more rounds of Fast-Food Stanislavski, it is at the very least a great exercise for everyone to make action lists on some objectives. The game is a wonderful means of translating the system into a playable and dynamic tool in the context of scene work.

## NEUTRAL SCENES

The final exercise involves many different facets of the Stanislavski system. By now students should have a pretty good grasp of the concept of superobjectives, objectives, and actions. But what of given circumstances, as well as the many facets of concentration and communication between actors in the context of a scene? This exercise gives students the opportunity to invest in several aspects of the system and experience the physical reality of playing out a scene with a partner. The concept of Neutral Scenes is brought to us by Robert Cohen, a distinguished teacher at the University of California, Irvine.[34]

The idea is simple. A relatively nondescript scene with no inherent plot or characters is assigned to pairs of students. They are then given scenarios that flesh out the scene. These scenarios are loaded. They provide characters and situations that are dynamic and filled with potential conflict and tension. But they are merely skeletons. They provide the opportunity for choices and decision making. The tissue and muscle that will make the scene come to life must be provided by the students through their imaginations. They have to devise the history of the characters' relationship, the location, as well as all the intangible factors that weigh on this particular moment. The more specific they are in what they decide, the more the scene will seem truthful and spontaneous. These are the two Neutral Scenes followed by a selection of scenarios. The scenarios are my own, and the instructor should feel welcome to devise new ones.

### Neutral Scene 1

A: Hi!
B: Hello.

A: How's everything?
B: Fine. I guess.
A: Do you know what time it is?
B: No. Not exactly.
A: Don't you have a watch?
B: Not on me.
A: Well?
B: Well what?
A: What did you do last night?
B: Nothing.
A: Nothing?
B: I said, nothing!
A: I'm sorry I asked.
B: That's all right

## Neutral Scene 2

A: Hi!
B: Hello.
A: You all right?
B: Yes.
A: Are you sure?
B: Yes, I'm sure. A little headache, that's all.
A: Oh, good. You want an aspirin?
B: No. Don't be so helpful, OK?
A: You are upset.
B: Good Lord!
A: OK, OK. I thought you might want to talk.
B: About what?
A: About anything.
B: I'm going away.
A: What do you mean?
B: I'm going away, that's all.
A: Where?
B: Not far. Don't get excited.
A: When?
B: Now.

## Scenarios for Neutral Scene 1

- A is female, B is male. At home on the day after a fight in which B walked out on A.
- A and B can be either sex. A bus station. B is a runaway from a juvenile counseling center. A is a counselor who has been looking for B.
- A and B are female. Breakfast table. A is the mother of B and a recovering alcoholic. She recently got full custody of her daughter, B.
- A and B are female. A has a crush on a guy and confided in B. A suspects B went on a date with him last night.
- A and B can be either sex. An office. A is B's boss. A recently fired B's best friend over an issue that was actually A's fault.
- A and B are male. Teammates on a baseball team. A just publicly acknowledged his homosexuality.
- A and B are female. Roommates. B found A's diary and read it. In it, A confessed that she has a crush on B.

## Scenarios for Neutral Scene 2

- A is female, B is male. A married couple at home. Late the previous night, B came home covered in blood with a cut on his hand and offered no explanation.
- A and B are male. Patrol partners at a police station. B has just concluded being interviewed by internal affairs regarding his shooting of a sixteen-year-old boy in an incident in which both officers were involved.
- A and B are female. A hospital. A is visiting her daughter, B, after B has been admitted after being date raped.
- A is male, B is female. B is a prostitute, and A is her pimp. A customer has just beaten up B, and A is cleaning her wounds.
- A is male, B is female. A's apartment. A and B are old friends. They have never been intimate, but there is a sexual tension between them. B just left her boyfriend, and A has offered to let her stay with him.
- A is male, B can be male or female. Backstage after an athletic

competition. A is B's father and coach. It is the state finals, and B just performed badly in the tournament.

- A is male, B is female. A breakfast table. A is B's stepfather. Last night A made a pass at B and was rebuffed.
- A and B are female. A is B's aunt and has had custody of B since her parents died. B just found out the drunk driver who killed them has been acquitted on a technicality.
- A and B can be either sex. B is a celebrity who has just been arrested for a DUI and is at the police station. A is his or her lawyer who has just secured the release on bail.
- A and B can be either sex. A homeroom. A and B are friends and lab partners. They both cheated on an assignment, but only B was caught. B is being expelled.

As I said, these scenarios are loaded in terms of given circumstances. The key is that the actors don't play into their own impressions of the archetypes or in some cases stereotypes and instead work to humanize and add dimension to the characters. They do this by building a history based on specific details. The only limits on this effort is the students' own imagination and their willingness to commit to the situation.

After a scene has been performed, it is important to ask the audience what they saw. What is the relationship? Who are they? What is going on? However, this is not charades, where the object of the game is to give clues to the onlookers. Instead, this feedback provides crucial insight into how effective the actors were in conveying the story by focusing on the situation. In working the scenes, the instructor needs to press the actors into articulating their actions and objectives and focus them on the given circumstances. Even if a character seems to be a "heavy" and driven by objectively selfish or morally objectionable motives, the onus is on the actor to find a justification for his or her behavior. No character acts in a way that he or she does not believe to be somehow right. The actor must look for the reasons for the behavior and play with an understanding that allows the actions to be human and truthful to the circumstances. The key is to embrace the first action of the scene and make adjustments based on the behavior of the scene partner. The beats come as the actors adjust to achieve their overall objective.

These exercises give actors the opportunity to get a handle on many of the crucial aspects of the Stanislavski system. But they are far from exhaustive. The earliest part of the system, including the controversial concept of affective memory, has yet to be explored. These are the aspects of Stanislavski's system that made its way to the United States and formed the basis of what is commonly referred to as Method acting. As such, they will be explored in the section on Lee Strasberg and the Americanization of the system. But next we turn to another Russian who amplified and extended the reach of what Stanislavski had established.

# PLATFORM 3: MICHAEL CHEKHOV

As we have previously noted, Michael Chekhov was a brilliant and gifted actor in both the Moscow Art Theatre and the First Studio, the more experimental wing of the MAT. He parted ways with Stanislavski over the nature of the actor's role. For Stanislavski, the play was sacrosanct and the actor's job was to use the clues provided by the playwright and acting technique to interpret the character in terms laid out by the text. Chekhov felt that the text was merely the starting point for the actor and that his role was as a creative artist, along the lines of a painter or sculptor. His task is to create something altogether new and original that enhances and could ultimately surpass the conception of the character as written. Chekhov embraced aspects of Stanislavski's system, citing the concept of units, objectives, and actions as his greatest accomplishment. But he also believed that the earliest part of the system, including the use of affective memory, constrained the actor to a vocabulary of behavior and expression limited to his own personal experience. He felt that the creation of compelling characters in a range of styles and milieus demanded a scope of creative possibilities outside the actor's own everyday understanding. He saw Stanislavski's methods, at least those employed at the MAT while Chekhov was a member, as inevitably leading toward naturalism. Chekhov believed that there was a link between the actor's imagination and physical self that could expand the compass of his habitual self in ways that could serve even the most extreme characterization.[35]

The dichotomy between Stanislavski and Chekhov is comparable to the split between the two burgeoning figures in psychology at the time, Freud and Jung. Freud saw the behavior of an individual as being dependent on the interrelation of various drives and repressions in a somewhat mechanistic model. Jung, however, saw the basis of human psychology as being the individual's relationship to a collective unconscious and a dreamscape of archetypes and shared experience. To access this well of creativity, Chekhov devised new exercises strongly influenced by the work of the scholar and philosopher Rudolf Steiner. However, when the censors of the recently established socialist state banned Steiner's work, Chekhov was deemed a dangerous artist and forced to emigrate. Compelled by the emerging events of World War II to move from France to England and, finally, to the United States, Chekhov headed a number of companies and studios in which he refined his techniques and exercises in an effort to provide actors with a means to liberate their imagination and unconscious creativity.

## THE OVERVIEW

From Steiner, Chekhov derived a view of the artist as having a higher ego. He saw this as a creative self that allowed the actor to create from a part of his being separate and distinct from his everyday nature. He likened this state to that of a painter in a moment of inspired creation or of an athlete immersed in the split seconds of his sport. This is a state that has been analyzed in depth in Mihaly Csikszentmihalyi's book *Flow: The Psychology of Optimal Experience*.[36] From the vantage point of this state, the actor remains in tune with the character and able to adjust and fine-tune individual moments in anticipation of the impact on an audience.

There are various determining factors over this self as it creates.

Ease is the concept that all actions onstage need to be performed with effortlessness. This is analogous to Stanislavski's emphasis on relaxation. But instead of merely saying "relax," Chekhov advocates performing actions such a sitting or reaching for an object with "a feeling of ease." He stipulates that even the most strenuous, violent, or comic actions must be performed without unnecessary tension in order for the audience to focus on the action itself and not the physical strain or the safety of the actor performing it. Form dictates that even the most muddled and chaotic character must be portrayed with a sense of precision and form. It advocates taking creative responsibility for the physical aspect of character and its impact on the audience.

Chekhov's techniques offer actors concrete means that allow actors to undertake even the most frenzied and ugly exchanges with an awareness of form. Beauty is a somewhat deceptive concept. It does not refer to a narcissistic or ego-driven notion of character. Rather, it implies the harmony and balance inherent to great works of art. It implies that the actor must take an aesthetic responsibility for his conception, much as a painter would for his work. Entirety or the feeling of the whole refers to the sense that in every instance, the actor must employ a conception of the whole of his creation. A monologue, scene, or entire play must convey this sense of wholeness and completeness. It thereby becomes a touchstone for the actor to reference the individual choices and moments of the role with a larger context that gives these instances meaning. While these concepts seem theoretical, Chekhov's techniques are, in fact, a practical and physical means to approaching a role.

## STARTING OFF

Chekhov's work is highly physical, and the technique requires participants to engage completely in each of the exercises. Students form a circle and perform a series of movements with a beginning, middle, and an end. As they explore each of the physical actions, they are invited to use different tempos. At first students are asked to expand their bodies as large as they can by reaching and stretching into the surrounding space. After they have performed the action three times, students then contract their bodies, folding in on themselves in a kind of fetal position to make their bodies as small as possible. Again after three repetitions, employing varying tempos, students explore physical tasks. As they perform each of the following tasks, again in a series of threes, they are told to bear in mind the concepts of ease, form, beauty, and entirety and, importantly, to support each of the movements with their breath. They are asked to imagine a heavy stone before them and to bend down and lift it over their heads. Next, they imagine a large object before them and push it forward along the ground. They then envision a rope and seize it to pull a weighted object toward them. Next, they take an imagined axe and split a log before them. Finally, they throw an imaginary ball across a great distance. These first movements serve as a warm-up.

## CENTERS, TEMPOS, AND MOVEMENT DYNAMICS

In this section, the space is cleared except for chairs and furniture around the periphery of the room. Students are invited to travel through the space comfortably, with an awareness of their own habitual ways of moving. They can walk through the space, sit, bend down to adjust a shoelace, or explore their standing posture. Next, as they move through the space, they are asked to imagine a center in the middle of their bodies, the region of their solar plexus. This center is to be imagined as a small sun from which all their movements emanate. This is their habitual center. After they have integrated the thought of this center, they are asked to change its quality and location and move with an awareness of the changing effect of their own physical perception as well as how they present themselves to the outside world.

- First, they are to imagine that the center has grown in size and weight and now contains a thick, gelatinous substance that moves slowly within a sphere. The center now resides in the seat of the pants. Students are now asked to perform the same vocabulary of movements with the altered dynamic. After they have explored the new center, they are instructed to let go of it and return to their habitual way of moving.

- Next, the center shrinks to the size of a ball bearing, becoming cold and hard and rotating quickly and moves to point directly between the eyebrows. Again, students move throughout the space, allowing this new center to inform their physical actions and perceptions of each other. Again, after a reasonable amount of time, they return to their habitual center.

- Now the center stretches and becomes tight and rigid, like an iron rod, and resides in the middle of the torso. Students explore how this image informs their psychological relationship to the space and to each other. After a period of exploration, the class assumes their habitual mode of movement and perception.

- Finally, the center elevates and becomes feather light, spinning and dancing erratically at a point about four inches above and in front of the students' faces.

These adjustments of the center can be augmented by other centers, and each can suggest a range of characteristics and psychologies to the student. The small hard center may suggest an intelligent, cunning, and calculating character looking to dominate his environment. The slow, oversized center may suggest a lazy, dull-witted character whose main drive is self-gratification. The centers represent broad strokes in determining a character's core and can be refined to a high degree. Characters' centers can also be shifted and adjusted in different scenes to respond to the dynamics of the contexts in which they find themselves. After the class has explored the centers collectively, it is a good idea to have them choose one or devise a new one and have them interact with their own individual centers.

In the next section, students are told to move around the space freely, aware of their own comfortable tempo or speed of movement.

After they have established the tempo, students are told to freeze in place. The instructor then assigns each student with a letter A, B, or C. After the students resume the movement, the instructor adjusts the tempo. For example, he tells the A's to move 30 percent faster, the B's to move 10 percent slower, and the C's, 70 percent slower. When the new tempos have been established, he again adjusts each of the groups' tempos to give every student the experience of a range of tempos. As in the previous exercise, the tempos themselves may suggest an internal state, such as impatience, resignation, fear, or contentment. The changing tempos also give the students an understanding of the divergence of inner tempos, as well as the inherent intentions and states of mind that produce them, which exist all around them in society at large.

In the final section, students move through the space as before with a sense of their own habitual dynamics. The instructor then invites them to explore four movement dynamics. While the dynamics may suggest certain tempos, students are asked to explore them in varying tempos and to observe the changes. The dynamics can be overtly explored, but eventually students should be instructed to internalize the dynamics and explore the residual sense of the dynamics without portraying them outwardly. In between, they are instructed to return to their everyday dynamic.

- In *molding*, students are asked to imagine that the air surrounding them has become thicker and offers resistance. As they move through it, their gestures leave traces and impressions in the thickening atmosphere. Every movement requires more effort and determination to perform. It also endows the body with more mass and solidity as it encounters the resistance.
- In *floating*, the body moves effortlessly. It is carried here and there by a supportive force that controls its movement, like a bottle in the ocean. The body now lacks mass and is buoyant and moves without a strong determination.
- In *flying*, students incorporate the sensation of soaring through space. The dynamic has a sense of freedom, and

while it entails effort, there is a quality of grace to the movement.

- In *radiating*, students explore the space with the notion that rays emanate from the body. Before any gesture or motion, these rays precede the physical action, and afterward, there is an echo of the movement.

After exploring the movement dynamics, students are invited to choose a center from those explored along with a tempo and dynamic. They move through the space and let the new elements define a character. They are then invited to give their character a name and profession. After a reasonable amount of time, they interact with each other in the context of a ten-year high school reunion. This gives students the opportunity to use the techniques in creating a character.

## QUALITIES

In contrast to the concept of finding an emotional basis for actions from the actor's own past, the principle of *affective memory* established by Stanislavski, Chekhov advocated the use of *qualities*. Simply put, the idea is to find a simple action and add to it a quality. For Chekhov, "the action is what, the quality is how."[37] For example: He opens the door with a quality of nervous apprehension. The quality has an emotional tone but is not motivated by a specific trigger. By focusing on the action and allowing the quality to color it, the actor begins to experience the emotion without needing to manufacture it internally.

The exercise that illustrates the principle is a simple improvisation. Two actors take the stage. A table, two chairs, a book or magazine, a backpack, keys, and a note are required. One actor sits by the table reading a book or magazine. The other actor enters from a doorway with a backpack and puts her keys on the table and the backpack on the vacant chair. She says hi and gets no response from the other actor. She then looks at a note on the table on which is written "John called," and exits through another door. These simple physical actions need to be performed precisely and in the correct order. After the actors have acquainted themselves with the scenario, qualities are added to the actions of the entering actor. The actor simply performs the same routine actions, but before doing so adds a quality to the movements. Here are some possible qualities:

1. Caution
2. Content
3. Suspicion
4. Resentment
5. Fear
6. Seduction
7. Silliness
8. Triumph
9. Mischief
10. Defeat

What is interesting about the exercise is the change in the perception of the audience. Nothing is physically different from one version of the scene to another. Yet once the scene is infused with emotional content through the qualities, the audience picks up cues and starts extrapolating about the relationship between the two actors. Is the reading actor an abusive lover? Is the entering actor concealing a secret? What is the importance of the note that is read? Through purely technical means the actors have created a dynamic relationship and added colors that have started to shape a story.

## ATMOSPHERES

In his concept of *atmosphere*, Chekhov creates a practical tool out of something that most actors take for granted. In every space we inhabit there exists an atmosphere that affects us on an emotional, physical, and aesthetic level. Our entire being responds to these atmospheres. Think of the calm of a wooded lakeside, the frenetic energy of a busy city street, or the solemn tranquility of a cathedral.

Our behavior and internal state are modulated by our interactions with these environments.

Chekhov advocates using the imagination to create these atmospheres on the stage as a means of linking the actor to the audience and shaping the actions of the characters. For Chekhov, the atmosphere is not merely a tone or a mood, but a dynamic force that when utilized by the actor leads him to nuances and specific reactions that enhance his work. As he stated, "Atmospheres enable the actor to create the element of the play and the part that cannot be expressed otherwise."[38] The atmospheres are inherent to the play and give the actor a partner and collaborator with which to impact the audience. An atmosphere can be fluid and shift based on the actions of those within in it, but if it is ignored, it undermines the world of the play.

The exercises on atmospheres are group improvisations. In the first part of the exercises, the actors allow the atmosphere to be established and work in harmony with it. First, the entire class is invited to explore the following atmospheres: a sunny beach, an art gallery, a subway platform on a hot summer day, a prison yard, a cathedral, and a kindergarten classroom. The second part introduces an intrusion that shifts the relationship to the atmosphere. Each improvisation involves roughly ten actors.

1. A bazaar in a third world country; a market place in an occupied country that has been racked by civil war and terrorist bombings. Actors may take the part of shopkeepers or citizens buying goods. The pervasive atmosphere is of imminent danger and anxiety. Into this atmosphere enters a political representative of the occupying country being given a tour by a military commander. He is on a fact-finding mission on the progress of the occupation and is oblivious, at least initially, to the atmosphere that surrounds him.

2. A rave party; a late night celebration. The actors create and respond to an atmosphere of ecstatic freedom and loss of inhibitions. Into this atmosphere comes an angry boyfriend looking for a girlfriend who has left him.

3. A picnic. In a serene outdoor environment, a group of friends

relax and loll on the grass enjoying themselves. The atmosphere is one of calm and content. Into this environment comes an overly aggressive panhandler. He or she is shabbily dressed and reeks of alcohol and urine.

In all the exercises, the atmosphere itself is as important an element as any particular actor. By evoking and drawing on the atmosphere, the individual actors have freed themselves to focus on their objectives and actions. The atmosphere works unconsciously on both the actors and the audience and provides a crucial means of sharing the story.

## INCORPORATION OF IMAGES, TRANSFORMATIONS

Chekhov found an alternative to the purely analytical basis for characterization. He cited Shakespeare, Dickens, and Michelangelo as artists from whose imagination beautiful and complex characters were formed and then liberated through creative means. He saw the actor as no less of a creator. He believed an image of the character could inspire and reveal its truthful behavior to the actor directly through the imagination. He advocated finding a clear picture of the character in one's mind and through a dialogue allowing the character to demonstrate his gestures and reveal the defining aspects of his nature. Gradually, this image of the character informs all the actor's movements and forms of expression. The key is that when performing the role, this mental image replaces the actor's own self-image. This allows a small actor to incorporate a large body, a young girl to become an old woman, a strong and healthy actor to transform into an invalid. This new body is like a suit of clothes that an actor can step into to change both the way she perceives the world and how she is perceived.

The exercise can be either done in class or students may prepare on their own and perform their results in class. The task is to find a strong image of a character and incorporate that image onto the actor's own body. It should be a clear character or archetype, such as "a vain young woman," "a ruthless soldier," or "a pompous old man." Students may draw characters from literature or from observation, but not from movies or television shows they have seen. They should explore the image until they can find simple physical actions or gestures that allow them to step into the character. Once they have found the one character, the second part of the assignment is to find its complete opposite. An old man may become a toddler, a vicious killer may change into a priest, and a wealthy politician could become a homeless beggar. The same image work is done for the second character. They then perform the one character transforming into the second. After they have performed the transformations individually, the students interact with each other as the first character. It is good to have a context such as museum or park for them to play with. When the instructor calls out a signal, all the characters transform and interact with one another once again.

## THE PSYCHOLOGICAL GESTURE

One of the most celebrated innovations of Chekhov's technique is also one of his most misunderstood. The *psychological gesture* is a means of preparation that enriches and adds dimension to the acting of a scene or a role. The term does not, however, refer to any overt gesture or expression used in performance or rehearsal. Chekhov himself reminded students, "Always keep in mind that the Psychological Gesture has nothing to do with various gestures the actor might use on the stage while rehearsing or performing."[39] The psychological gesture is a way of activating the actor's body, will, and emotions toward what the character is doing or experiencing in the play.

Chekhov found the concept through his work. While rehearsing the part of Strindberg's Erik IV, Chekhov was drilling the director, Yevgeny Vakhtangov, with questions. Vakhtangov, a brilliant director in his own right, suddenly jumped up and exclaimed, "That is your Erik. Look! I am now within a magic circle and cannot break through it!"[40] The character's impotence, fear, and suffering all seemed contained in this image. Vakhtangov's powerful and emotionally committed gesture became the inspiration for Chekhov's acclaimed performance. By finding the image of the character and seeing the character's experience, we can find an imaginative expression of these goals and actions in physical terms.

Some examples are "I am climbing the ladder of my own ambition, but I never get high enough," or "I am protecting those around me," or "I am being crushed by my family's expectations." When the actor has found a central gesture for a character, or for even one scene or action, she may temper it with different qualities and use different tempos until it truly activates her will, feelings, and body. She then performs it over and over, each time internalizing it until the movement has entirely penetrated her, but no outward sign of it remains. When she then acts in the scene, the residue and resonance of the gesture will powerfully affect her acting. It can articulate a character's unconscious. For example a character's words may be stoic in the face of emotionally devastating news. But if the actor has done a psychological gesture of the character falling down a great chasm and flailing helplessly, we will get both the stoic cover of the character and the emotional impact that lies beneath. It is a means of exploring more than just the surface expression of a character.

As an exercise, I divide the class into a group A and a group B. I tell the As to devise their own individual gesture that is open and free and permeated with a sense of content and goodwill. The B's work on a gesture that is aggressive and domineering and controlling. Students will need time to explore their own gestures and should be encouraged to find a gesture with a beginning, middle, and an end. Once all the students have devised their gestures, they then internalize them and walk around the room. After a few moments, the class sits down and in pairs of A and B, they perform the following improvised scenarios. In each case, the pairs leave the room to do their individual gestures and then come back in and perform the scenario.

1. A is an office manager and has called B into his or her office to fire them.
2. A and B are on a blind date.
3. A is a politician who has just made a big speech in which he or she admitted an affair, and B is their campaign manager.

4. At a bank, B is applying for a loan from A.

5. A is in a doctor's office getting a diagnosis from B.

6. A is being interrogated in a murder investigation by B.

7. A is interviewing for a job at a fast-food restaurant with B, the manager.

8. B is a priest hearing the confession of A.

In some cases, the psychological gestures reinforce the inherent status dynamics of the scenarios. In other cases, they work in conflict, creating another level of tension. Each gesture will try to assert itself in the scene, which creates an exquisite tension. Both the actors and audiences will find that using psychological gesture grounds the players in the relationship so that they don't need to work at establishing a point of view. From the start of the scene, they have a foundation to rely on that colors all their individual actions and allows them to react freely with their partner.

## FINAL SCENE

The final task of the platform is to integrate all these component parts into a fully realized and rehearsed scene. We return again to the neutral scenes. Here the instructor is faced with a choice. He may revisit the original scenes, allowing the new tools to deepen and inform the situation and actions. Or the instructor may allow the students themselves to determine the characters, the context, and the action of a new scene. Both approaches have their merits. In the first case, students can use the techniques to build on a foundation already established. If the new scene is chosen, they can assert themselves and their imaginations in creating the characters and the scenario to animate the words. In both cases, students are invited to draw from the various means that Chekhov provides, including psychological gesture, qualities, movement dynamics, atmospheres, centers, and tempos. The idea is to enlist students in a creative process, not merely an interpretive one. The new scene is brief, but affords a range of opportunities.

## Neutral Scene 3

> A: Please.
> B: I can't.
> A: Just try.
> B: I don't know.
> A: Please.
> B: Can you?
> A: Don't even.
> B: But.
> A: No.
> B: You're mad.
> A: Please.
> B: All right.
> A: Ready.
> B: You know.
> A: What's that?
> B: Here.
> A: OK.
> B: Great.

In working with the scenes, the instructor should emphasize the opportunities afforded by the various aspects of Chekhov's method. Students can be intimidated by possibilities. It is not unreasonable to think: I have to figure out the given circumstances, I have to decide on my character's objectives and my actions, and now I have to come up with all these other decisions about the atmospheres, and internal dynamics of the character? But that is the wrong way to look at it. As we have stated, the goal of storytelling is to find the ways to maximize a scene's impact on the audience. The techniques of Chekhov provide the actor with concrete means to enhance that impact. Actors should never permit these techniques to devolve into a laundry list of tasks they have to do to make a scene work. Instead, Chekhov's work offers a means to extend the palette of what an actor can use in approaching a role. His techniques can provide a way into a role when the actor is blocked or has hit a wall in his or her process. The expanded techniques serve to anchor the actor in the world and values of the scenario. The purpose is to reassert the actor's role as a creative artist and to enlist his or her imaginative faculties to their full potential and not merely "get it right."

# PLATFORM 4: MONOLOGUES

> Emphasis on monologues is a total evasion of acquiring an acting technique.
>
> —*Uta Hagen*[41]

To concur with the noted teacher and actress, the prevailing use of monologues as the primary vehicle for presenting and assessing talent is one of the many problems we face in the profession. For one thing, monologues necessarily invite many of the qualities that undermine effective acting: an emphasis on self, the desire to show off, and the need to gain approval. It is also asking a lot of an actor to stand in an unfamiliar room in front of people he has just met and talk to invisible characters in an imagined location with no context to support him. Having said that, the use of the principles of storytelling can be of tremendous value to the actor approaching this necessary evil. It is my belief, however, that work on monologues should be introduced as the last step in a storytelling curriculum. The search for a monologue nevertheless must start much earlier, as the connection between the actor and the monologue should be intimate and impassioned. It therefore becomes a parallel process.

The first step in selecting a monologue is to understand the varying nature of its construction. Monologues can take the form of speeches in which a character addresses another character in the play, they may be soliloquies in which a character speaks to himself out loud, or they may be direct address in which a character speaks to the audience. The three forms present distinctly different challenges. In the first instance, the actor must use a great deal of imagination and concentration to specifically create things and people that are not there. In the second instance, the actor must make an unfamiliar activity, talking to one's self out loud, seem natural and compelling dramatically. Direct address at least affords the actor the opportunity of talking to actual people, but this is complicated by the potential discomfort and aversion of those people to participate in the scene. It is best to be aware of these challenges when choosing a monologue.

The most important aspect in selecting a piece is that it must be compelling to the actor. Whether humorous or dramatic, it must create excitement and enthusiasm in the actor as she imagines herself performing it. Just as the initial storytelling exercise was predicated on finding a connection to a piece of text, the monologue must hold a personal connection for the actor. That immediate connection will provide the foundation for all the work that is to follow. It also opens the first door to the storytelling approach, the desire to share something meaningful with an audience. A series of questions need to be asked. If the monologue is part of a scene, does it stand on its own? Is it too dependent on the context of the scene from which it comes to make sense and compel an audience? Does it have a strong and clear beginning and ending? Relatively speaking, the monologue is only a snapshot of the character from the play, which is itself only a snapshot from the entire life of that character before and after the play begins. One must be objective in order to see if what is compelling about the character is reflected in the brief monologue, or if it is reliant on the entire story of the play.

There are countless monologue books that provide short pieces that are meant to be self-contained stories. The danger of these pieces is that they are devoid of the kind of rich characterization and context that a well-crafted play affords. The onus is on the actors to fill in all the given circumstances with their own imaginations. But the construction of the monologues often betrays such efforts because they are not written to encompass anything other than rudimentary characterization. They can be clever, amusing, or emotional, but I have found that many of them reflect more on the facility of the writer than any true depth of character.

If actors are to use monologue books, it is best to use them as a road map. If an actor is struck by the tone or content of an excerpted monologue, the burden is on the actor to then go and find the full play. By doing so, the actor not only uncovers the given circumstances that inform the monologue, he may also find other potential pieces in the play. An actor may also discover a playwright whose other works yield even more possible monologues for interpretation. What is crucial is that an actor recognizes in the voice of a character or a writer something that speaks to him so that he is compelled to share it with an audience. Movies are another potential source for monologues. However, the obstacle is that actors have such strong visual associations with the original interpretation. If an actor is to choose a monologue from a movie, it is best to treat it as a work of literature and try and divorce the writing from the filmed version so that the actor is free to make his own choices.

There is also a wealth of potential monologue material to be found outside specifically dramatic literature. Novels, documentaries, and poetry can yield rich and unique pieces that can be dynamically interpreted. Verbatim testimony in legal trials or sections of nonfiction accounts can offer chilling insights into actual living breathing human beings. The bottom line is that interpreting monologue requires an enormous amount of work, much of it solitary. It is crucial to start the journey with something compelling enough to get you to the final destination.

We will discuss some approaches to interpreting and performing monologues within a storytelling context in the final platform of this chapter. What is important to remember now is that the time spent searching for a monologue that is exciting and enjoyable to the actor will easily match or surpass the time spent working on the piece. Ultimately, any actor should possess a selection of monologues that can be used in accordance with different contexts. Any actor who tries to cram or learn a monologue on the fly from a source that holds no inherent meaning for her is greatly reducing her chances for success.

# PLATFORM 5: LEE STRASBERG

> He was a gigantic genius, a consummate master teacher, but a flawed man.
>
> —*Madeleine Thornton-Sherwood, Actors Studio Member*[42]

> Along with Stanislavski and Brecht, he was one of the major names in twentieth-century theatre.
>
> —*Viveca Lindfors, Actors Studio Member*[43]

> If he is a genius at anything, it is in the fine art of inspiring insecurity.
>
> —*Gordon Rogoff, former Actors Studio Administrative Director*[44]

> Strasberg will not work out ideas with any of the rest of us. He assumes that he knows everything and that we know nothing. He plunges blindly ahead, even when proved wrong as he has been in the past. In the role that he has given himself, he assumes the power of the minder of souls and prober into the unconscious.
>
> —*Robert Lewis, Cofounder, Actors Studio*[45]

Lee Strasberg was many things to many people.[46] No one, however, can question his impact, for better or worse, on a generation of American acting. By trade a wigmaker, Lee Strasberg as a young man was an inveterate theatergoer with a passion for great acting. He mused eloquently on the early impressions made on him by Laurette Taylor and Jacob Ben-Ami. Though he received no formal theatre education, he was a bibliophile and amassed an incredible library of texts and possessed a vast collection of theatre memorabilia that included a lock of Eleanor Duse's hair. He was a young student of theatre in New York just at the time that a great wave was about to crash upon the theatre scene.

The arrival of the Moscow Art Theatre tour in 1923 proved a revelation to this generation of young actors and directors. The focused, almost unconscious natural behavior of the ensemble and the truthfulness of their emotional expression stood in stark contrast to the stylized performances in the star-centered comedies and melodramas of Broadway. With the concrete example of this new style of acting, a desire grew for the training and methods that had produced it. Strasberg was among the students of Richard Boleslavsky and Maria Ouspenskaya at the American Laboratory Theatre, where actors who had worked firsthand with the master were teaching the earliest formulations of Stanislavski's system. At the same time, essays on the system by Sudakov and Vakhtangov and other contemporaries of Stanislavski were becoming available, though not yet translated from their original Russian.

Inspired by this new approach, Strasberg, along with his colleagues Harold Clurman and Cheryl Crawford, sought to create an American ensemble modeled after the Moscow Art Theatre. Because of his extensive research and broad knowledge of theatre, Strasberg was placed in charge of training the Group Theatre. He drew from his experience of the system as gleaned from the translated writings as well as from the teachings of Boleslavsky and Ouspenskaya. He utilized animal exercises, improvisations, concentration and object exercises, and, most significantly, affective memory. Throughout his long career as a teacher, a director, and later as an actor himself, Strasberg relied on affective memory as not merely an important element of, but as the very essence of the Method, which came to be known as his adaptation of Stanislavski's system. While others, including Stanislavski himself, ultimately moved away from a reliance on the technique, Strasberg obstinately insisted on its importance. It was in fact a large contributor to the fractures that caused him to resign from the Group in 1937.

After leaving the Group Theatre, Strasberg had a long sojourn from directing, which he filled with teaching under the auspices of Erwin Piscator at the New School for Social Research. There, confronted with a diversity of approaches including Piscator's own view of epic theatre and objective acting, Strasberg continued to believe his approach to be the crucial means for creating emotionally truthful acting onstage. In 1947, Elia Kazan, Robert Lewis, and Cheryl Crawford founded the Actors Studio. Far from a conventional theatre school, it was designed as a workshop for professional actors to maintain and develop their craft in a supportive environment under the tutelage of two of the foremost directors of the times. It became a magnet for some of the most dynamic young actors of the era. However, the success of Kazan and Lewis forced their frequent absence, and out of necessity, the fledgling studio brought in Strasberg.

In moderating his twice-weekly sessions at the studio, Strasberg reasserted the emphasis on the internal processes of the actor. To his previous exercises, he added the "private moment," which was an adaptation of Stanislavski's concept of public solitude: the ability to perform in public as if one is completely alone. These exercises forced actors to confront their own self-consciousness and lose their inhibitions by revealing their intimate selves in a public forum. Actors would dance, sing, prance in front of a mirror, even cover themselves in talc as a means of exploring their own intensely private behavior. But the essence of the Method, what Strasberg saw as the key to authentically truthful behavior, was affective memory. Strasberg became a strong advocate for psychoanalysis as a means for actors to unblock themselves and access the reservoir of their own emotional pasts. Having rediscovered emotionally charged episodes, actors could then create an index of emotions that they could summon at will in accordance with the demands of a play. He stressed that remembered emotions were more valuable to actors than spontaneous feeling arising from circumstances because they could be controlled and adapted. "Remembered emotion is something that the actor can create and repeat; without that the thing is hectic," he said.[47]

In my classes, I focus on specific aspects of Strasberg's approach; observation, concentration, relaxation, and affective memory.

## OBSERVATION

As a means of starting off, I have the entire class form two lines facing each other roughly three feet apart. The instructions are simple: observe every detail of your partner's appearance. The actors have approximately five minutes to concentrate and catalogue all the details of the person in front of them. After the allotted time, I instruct the two lines to turn away from each other. I then face one line and I interrogate, one after the other, the person facing away about the appearance of their partner who stands before me. No matter how specific and emphatic I give the directions, I am always amazed at what the vast majority misses. Simple questions—such as What is written on your partner's shirt? Is your partner wearing makeup? or What color are your partner's eyes?—will be answered by pauses or wild guesses. Once students become aware of their lack of concentration in the task, partners can be switched and the task repeated, only this time with one minute allowed for the observation. The exercise is a way of jump-starting the class's use of concentration and sensitivity to detail.

## OBJECT TRANSFORMATIONS / SENSE MEMORY

Now that the importance of focused concentration has been demonstrated, it is useful to move into physical concentration through object transformations. The actors sit in a circle. The first actor imagines an object and through sensory detail interacts with it. It is important for the object not to be arbitrary, but a very specific object from the actor's own experience. The actor focuses on the texture, the weight, and the feel of the object and then recalls his specific sensory relationship to the object as he uses it. He then hands the object to the actor on the right. If that actor isn't clear what the object is, the first actor must continue the interaction until it is clear, acknowledged by a nod from the second actor. This actor then takes the object and interacts with it and then transforms it into a different object and hands it to the next actor in the circle. The process is then repeated around the circle. The trap of the exercise is that actors will put their energy into showing what the object is. Having a simple, concentrated interaction with the object is a more efficient means of communicating. The exercise is an excellent primer for concentration and imagination and further illustrates the need for doing, not showing.

# RELAXATION / AFFECTIVE MEMORY

While Strasberg performed this exercise in a one-on-one format, I've found it expedient and yet valuable to do it as a group. First of all, students are instructed to sit in a chair in a comfortable position that would permit them to fall asleep if they so chose. The class is advised that at the end of the affective memory, the instructor will tap them each on the shoulder and hand them an index card from which they will read some dialogue aloud.

The lights are dimmed and the instructor, in a calm and quiet voice, leads them through the relaxation exercise. Students are instructed to focus on their breath and scan their body for any tension. Starting at the feet, students imagine the muscles, ligaments, and small bones that support their full weight and carry them through all the activities in their day. As they inhale, they are told to tense and relax the feet and ankles and roll them around. As they exhale, they let any residual tension melt away into the floor. Slowly, they are instructed to move their attention upward into the calves, the knees, the hamstrings, and buttocks. As they move through each group of muscles, students again scan for tension and using the breath as a soothing balm, release the tension from their bodies. It is important to focus on specific areas of habitual tension as they move through their physical selves: the sphincter, the abdominal muscles, and all the large and small muscle groups along the spine that subtly adjust to keep us upright. Students move into the arms and again squeeze and relax the hands and rotate the wrists to locate and release tension. As they move into the neck and shoulders, they are invited to imagine strong and soothing hands massaging away the tension. As the students move their attention into their heads, Strasberg advocates paying particular attention to areas of mental tension.

> . . . the areas of the blue nerves, on the side of the temples. In the effort we make to think, these areas use much more energy than they need, and therefore create tension. Another area that we have found equally important is the bridge of the nose, leading into the eyelids. Here again, there is tension because these areas are very automatic in their response-the eyes are active all the time. We

simply suggest to the actor that he let the energy ooze out of the eyelids. It works because when you start to relax, you literally feel like almost dropping, so much energy is let out. The third area is that leading along the side of the nose, those thick muscles that lead into the mouth and chin. These areas, by the way, are the tensest and the most active, because they're the seat of habit. . . . These three areas are the seat of mental tension, and when these areas are relaxed, the tension disappears.[48]

The muscles of the jaw, along the scalp, and behind the ears also deserve attention as the students focus with increasing specificity on whatever slight areas of tension may remain. When the class has moved through their entire physical selves, they are invited to breathe deeply and let the exhalations remove any last tension. Now as they breathe in, they are encouraged to let sound emerge from this newly relaxed condition. The sound is not predetermined, but allowed to arise from the opened state of each individual actor. After allowing the sounds to emerge, the instructor tells the students to again focus on their breath. The next step is to focus their awareness. The instructor asks them to see if they can find the awareness of their own heartbeat. Next, they are asked to identify three specific sounds outside the room.

In this state of relaxed, yet focused awareness, the class now embarks on the affective memory exercise. The instructor calmly invites the students to enter into their memory and return to the time and place where it occurred. They are reassured that it is a memory and in the past and therefore safe. The instructor now asks a series of questions. What time of year is it? What does the air feel like? Is there a smell? What colors do you see as you look around? What objects could you reach out and touch? What sounds do you hear in this place? As the instructor slowly asks these questions, it is important to remind the class to keep breathing. The instructor continues to ask specific questions: What clothes are you wearing in this place? How do they feel on your body? If you could run your hand along a surface what would it feel like? Is it clean? What time of day is it? What is the quality of the light? What does the ground feel like? Can you make out a voice? Are you close to a door? A window?

What textures can you see around you? These questions should be asked calmly and slowly as a means of evoking the reality of the remembered past. After the questions, the instructor invites the students to simply be in this remembered place and to allow the awareness of what it means to be here. He then walks around the room, gently taps each student on the shoulder, and hands them an index card to read. He instructs them to read the words simply from whatever state they are in. On the cards are written the following:

- Please, I can't . . . I just need some time by myself. I don't know why . . . please.
- Don't. Just don't. I can't see you right now.
- It's not you. It's me. I'm sorry. I just can't . . . I'm sorry.
- You don't know me. You never did. Get out. Just go.
- I don't want to talk to you right now. OK?
- Why? I just want to know why.
- It's nothing. I just . . . Never mind.
- No, no, I'm fine. Really. I'll be fine.
- I thought you would understand. I guess I was wrong.
- Why do you even care? I'm such a . . .
- I don't care. Oh God, I just don't care anymore.
- What is wrong with you? Do you just not get it?

The point of the dialogue is to see how an emotional state colors language, even language that is nonspecific and that is unrelated to any explicit context. It also reaffirms that the point is not merely to evoke emotion for its own sake, but rather to evoke emotion that can then be released through words. After the dialogue part of the exercise, the students are told once again to focus on their breath, to bring their consciousness back into the present, and to gradually bring their awareness back to their bodies in the space. When they are ready they can open their eyes.

When everyone has left the exercise behind and come back into the shared space, I ask the class to move the chairs into a circle to discuss their experience. For some, the memory will have been clearly evoked and strong emotions produced. For others, the exercise will have been utterly fruitless. Still others will lie somewhere in between. This is not unusual. Strasberg himself had varying results with affective memory. He specified that memories should be at least seven years old so that they were less immediate and more malleable. That is not always possible for young actors, however. Sometimes different memories have to be explored before an actor finds a useable trigger. For other relatively uninhibited actors at the studio, Strasberg didn't advocate the use of affective memory. The exercise is nonetheless a useful starting point for a discussion of the use and production of emotion onstage.

Strasberg differed from other noted teachers of his generation in his strict adherence to the technique of affective memory. Stella Adler advocated the use of *substitution*, whereby the actor finds equivalent personalizations of the given circumstances as a means of giving the text its proper emotional context. The famous actress and teacher Uta Hagen used *transferences*, whereby she would distill an emotional experience to an internal *personal object* or image that would serve as a trigger to an emotion. However, she also warned that "[y]ou will need to supply personal psychological realities only when direct contact with the events, the objects, and your partners fails to stimulate you, when the imagination alone fails to support your specific actions during the moment-to-moment give and take which will prove that you are alive onstage."[49]

Strasberg based his interpretation on the work of Ivan Pavlov, the famed Russian psychologist who described conditioned responses. The goal in Strasberg's application is to take what may be a forty-minute preparation and repeat it so that it may then take twenty minutes and keep repeating the process until it takes no more than a minute. At that point, the actor uses the affective memory directly in performance. He does his preparation in the midst of the scene and evokes his own personal emotional state apart from, but in service to the given circumstances. This was the "dropping out" of the scene that some of the Group actors found so frustrating. Robert Lewis, Strasberg's colleague in the Group, put it thus, "One of the dangers of the wrong use of affective memory is the blindness— to say nothing of deafness and paralysis in general—that happens when the actor tries to hang on to the emotion that he receives from his emotional memory exercise, which makes it impossible for him to absorb and create the author's life going on in the scene. This is pathology, not art."[50]

The danger in the technique is to see feeling emotion as the ultimate goal. In fact, it is only the beginning point. That kernel of feeling must be shaped by the circumstances and actions of the characters. Even Vakhtangov, who formed much of Strasberg's theoretical basis, recognized this: "In life a man who weeps is concerned about restraining his tears—but the actor journeyman does just the opposite. Having read the remark of the author (He Weeps), he tries with all his might to squeeze out tears."[51] Andre Belgrader, a renowned director and a teacher of mine, once said aptly "a drunk doesn't try to walk like a drunk."[52] What he meant was that the drunk tries to walk a straight line, but his intoxication is an obstacle. It is the same way with emotion onstage. We are conditioned from a young age to be in control of our emotions. A character is thereby more apt to put his or her energies into maintaining composure and suppressing the emotion than giving it full expression. The emotion is often an obstacle to the character's real objectives in a scene. The emotion can also be an action in service to an objective, such as to get pity or to be feared. But it is never an end in itself. Being able to access our own storehouse of emotions is nonetheless a valuable starting point to truthful acting.

Much of the controversy regarding Strasberg lay in the nature of the Actors Studio. From its inception, the studio was meant as a laboratory where professionals could work on themselves and their craft, not as a conservatory for training actors. Strasberg saw himself as a moderator, not a teacher, and although he used specific techniques, he spent much of the time in his sessions critiquing individual actors' processes. Unlike the Moscow Art Theatre, which started as a producing entity and later developed its famous system of training, the Actors Studio was never meant to be a producing organization. In fact, the one season of plays produced by the studio was met with a decidedly mixed reaction by the public. Lacking the proving ground of a working ensemble to use and refine the techniques, the studio's focus inevitably shifted to the individual actor. While this served to empower actors in film, which required a microcosmic level of emotional availability and truth, it suffered in theatre, where the approach to emotion is more macrocosmic. Highly personalized emotions are less crucial to a play than is sensitivity to the overall story and circumstances that require precisely the right feeling at the right moment in service to the play's impact on an audience. By working on the entire play as opposed to pieces of it, the actors understand a larger context apart from their own sense of truth and find how the circumstances inform the emotions on a moment-to-moment basis. No doubt recognizing the importance of this connection, the Actors Studio recently announced the launch of their own three-year MFA conservatory program.

## PLATFORM 6: SANFORD MEISNER

Sanford Meisner was a successful actor in New York when the Moscow Art Theatre made its debut. He was invited to join the Group Theatre and trained under Lee Strasberg. He acted in some of their most famous productions, including *Awake and Sing* and *Waiting for Lefty*, which he also codirected. He was present when Stella Adler made her famous return from Paris with a detailed description of the system as taught by Stanislavski. He was schooled in Michael Chekhov's techniques by Chekhov himself. There was virtually no one in America in a better position to explain and utilize these burgeoning techniques than Meisner. It is fascinating, then, that when Meisner turned to teaching at the Neighborhood Playhouse, which was to be his home for over thirty years, he developed a radically new and different technique of training actors.[53]

Perhaps because of his direct experience with these techniques as an actor, Meisner came to realize that one of the most compelling aspects of live theatre was the apparently spontaneous interaction of real human beings. This was for him the essence of acting, not the individual actor's ability to access and use his own psychological history. Meisner was much more interested in creating real interaction between actors in the context of the play's circumstances. For Meisner, it was all about the doing. "The foundation of acting is the reality of doing," he said.[54] He would ask his students to count the number of lightbulbs in the room or to add in their heads two very large numbers. The correct answer was not his goal. Instead, he pointed out that in doing these simple tasks, students were not doing so as "characters," nor were they pretending to do them. Immersion in the act of doing leads to a loss of self-consciousness and abandonment of theatrical cliché. This concept of placing reality at the core of one's work became a hallmark of Meisner's technique.

Meisner's most famous exercise is the word repetition game. It is also widely misunderstood. Its goal is to start with simple observation and create a connection between actors. From that connection, the actors become aware of minute changes in behavior and act on impulses that arise from their own instincts. "To transfer the point of concentration outside of yourself," he said, "is a big battle won."[55] The repetition exercise forces actors to deal with the reality that is confronting them in the form of their partner. They are also confronted by their own need to shape and control the interaction. But Meisner is adamant about letting the impulses define the exchange and not the actor's need to be interesting or to create variety. "Don't do anything until something happens to make you do it"[56] was a mantra in his class. To the progression of the repetition game, Meisner adds an *independent activity*, his adaptation of Stanislavski's concept of public solitude. He also introduces the use of emotion in the form of *preparation*.

## PREPARATION

Meisner's use of preparation was a means to enter a scene with a live emotion. However, once the scene begins, the emotional state is subject to change as the actor interacts with the partner. Emotion for Meisner was not something that needed to be grafted into the middle of a scene, but rather was a starting point from which the actor proceeded organically within the given circumstances. "Don't come in empty," he said. "Preparation is what you start with. Preparation is to acting what warming up the motor is to driving a car on a cold day."[57] Meisner advocated using whatever personal preparation allows the actor to enter into a scene in the appropriate emotional state.

But rather than evoking specific memories, he encouraged using the imagination and finding emotion through fantasy. "Dr. Freud maintains that all fantasy comes either from ambition or sex," Meisner said.[58] In order to self-stimulate oneself into an emotional state, he suggested free associating from the actor's own given circumstances: If I come in elated, maybe I just got the phone call from my agent that I landed a huge role. If I come in devastated, perhaps I imagine catching my lover with someone else. The challenge is not to demonstrate emotion. This preparation only lasts a moment. Once the actor enters the scene, he interacts moment to moment with the scene partner. The emotion is merely the underlying tone. "The text is like a canoe," Meisner says, "and the river on which it sits is the emotion. The text floats on the river. If the water of the river is turbulent, the words will come out like a canoe on a rough river. It all depends on the flow of the river which is your emotion."[59]

While the following exercise is not specifically Meisner's, it uses his technique of preparation to activate the text. Students pair up and memorize the following dialogue by rote without inflection or intention:

A: I love you.
B: You do?
A: You didn't know that?
B: I do now.

Students will speak the dialogue to each other, but before doing so, each actor does a preparation. This entails fantasizing a scenario that could make her feel a certain way. It could be angry, joyful, sad, or afraid. There are no limits. The actors don't share with one another the emotions they are preparing or their own fantasy scenarios. They simply say the first line with the emotion behind it. However, they must stay connected to their partners so that they are observing and responding to the others' emotion as well. This thereby creates tensions and dynamics as the different emotional preparations propel the actors to interact. The key is to not cling to the emotion that the actor has prepared, but rather to respond to the partner. This short scene becomes lifeless if the actors are merely reiterating their preparation instead of reacting to the flesh-and-blood person in front of them. Each pair should try a number of different preparations and observe the dynamics of the different combinations.

When approaching a text, Meisner advocates learning the text by rote and reading it with a partner mechanically, without any intonation. The idea is to approach the text as something raw and unfixed, unencumbered by preconceived choices and readings. Knowing the given circumstances, the actors find emotional preparations and then react off each other, almost improvisatorially. In this way, the score of the scene is found not through cold analysis, but through dealing with a flesh-and-blood partner. "Don't pick up cues," Meisner demanded, "pick up impulses."[60] By working this way, an actor can return to the same scene with the same circumstances and always be finding new things. He also recommended the use of "particularizations." He defined it as such, "It's your personal example chosen from your experience or your imagination which emotionally clarifies the cold material of the text."[61] The particularization gives an actor a means into a particular moment in a play and was taken from Stanislavski's use of the "as if." For example, if I am in a scene in which my lover is humiliating me, my imagination can inform me to feel as if I am a five-year-old child being reprimanded in front of my entire school class. Particularization is a rehearsal tool that allows the actor to find rich associations that add specific and individual colors and shadings to a text.

Meisner also believed that character is defined not externally but internally. "For the most part, character is an emotional thing. The internal part of character is defined by how you feel about something."[62] In this way, our fears, desires, and attitudes toward sources we encounter create the character. This stands in seeming contrast to Michael Chekhov's work. However, if we remember the emphasis both men place on imagination, we realize that for both, character is the result of an imaginative extrapolation of impulses picked up intuitively from the text. For Meisner, everything in acting could be found through doing. In approaching his techniques, it is best to build simply from the foundation of repetition.

## THE WORD REPETITION GAME

To start, everyone in the class finds a partner and sits in chairs opposite each other about three feet apart. I've found it's best to designate each pair as A and B. It is a good idea to demonstrate with one pair, and then let the rest of the class attempt it.

Both partners observe each other. A starts and states an observation about B, such as "You are wearing hoop earrings." In the first incarnation of the game, B repeats exactly what she hears without adding any inflection or line reading, "You are wearing hoop earrings." A and B progress through the game, repeating exactly what they hear five or six times. After this has been demonstrated and the rest of the class begins, the instructor circulates through the room making sure that the partners aren't purposefully manipulating the readings to create variety. It may seem ridiculous at first and is very mechanical, but as Meisner says, "It is the basis for something." It is the start of a connection from which authentic impulses will emerge.

In the next stage, B starts and A answers the repetition in the first person as in "I am staring at you." As they progress this time, B is allowed to respond subjectively from what he observes about A.

B: You are staring at me.
A: I am staring at you.
B: You are staring at me.
A: I am staring at you.
B: You are trying not to laugh.
A: I am trying not to laugh.

> B: You are trying not to laugh.
> A: I am trying not to laugh.
> B: You are laughing.
> A: I am laughing.
> B: Now you're blushing.
> A: Now I'm blushing.

It is important to stress that every shift is based on an observable change in the partner. While it is spoken from B's point of view, it is outwardly focused. "I am uncomfortable" is not an observation of the partner, while "You are making me uncomfortable" is. After the class has practiced this next stage, they can reverse roles so that A responds from a subjective point of view.

After they have practiced both ways, they are both given license to depart from the repetition only as they observe a change in the partner. Now the interaction starts to resemble human conversation. The actors' own instincts determine the flow of the dialogue. Everything is predicated on observable behavior. If the partner is annoying or inert or even silent, that triggers a response that becomes part of the exchange. While the exercise may produce discomfort at first, if the actors are responsive to what they see as well as their own impulses, they will discover the basis of what underlies truthful communication. It is up to the instructor to help the actors realize when they are merely cataloguing surface facts instead of focusing on the actual shifts that arise. Actors also need to be made sensitive to these shifts, as many of us are unaccustomed to observing and being observed so specifically. The game serves a dual purpose. It focuses all the attention of the actor on the partner and acquaints him with the impulses that arise in response. But it also creates a muscle memory of an actual spontaneous moment-to-moment exchange that provides a template for truthful acting.

## INDEPENDENT ACTIVITY

The next step is to introduce into the word repetition game an *independent activity*. Meisner used the independent activity as a means to displace the self-awareness of the actors so that real behavior can emerge. It is a way of focusing concentration and using "doing" to free actors' instinctive impulses. Meisner described it thus, "The independent activity must be difficult, truly difficult, and the reason why you do it has to have a consuming reality for you."[63] One actor is alone in the room doing the activity, and then the other knocks at the door. The first actor goes to the door and opens it, letting the other actor in the room. He or she then resumes the activity, and at this point, based on the observed behavior, the two begin the repetition game. The activity can be anything that is achievable in the space, but it must be difficult if not impossible to do, and there has to be a compelling reason for doing it.

By way of example, Meisner takes a Manhattan phone book and hands it to an actor: "Last week, you met a beautiful girl at a party and she said, 'I'm having a party next Saturday night, and if you want to come to it, my family is in Europe, so you can stay all night' . . . Now, you wrote her name and address down on a slip of paper but you lost it. Fortunately, you remember her name. It's K. Z. Smith, and she lives in Manhattan on the East Side in the upper Seventies. Now, do you have a good reason to look up her address?"[64] Looking up a 'Smith' among the thousands in Manhattan is a difficult task and the prospect of staying alone with a beautiful young woman is a compelling reason for the actor. If it weren't, it would be the actor's responsibility to find an activity and a reason that is.

This again evokes Meisner's preferred use of fantasy to memory. The fantasy must be of an appropriate scale as well as being affecting to the actor. Diffusing a bomb is an activity with a huge imperative element, but it is not personally meaningful to most actors and is of an almost comically heightened nature. On the other side, merely balancing a checkbook is not a strong enough pull on the actor. He needs to activate it by imagining that his debit card was just refused and he must find out why before an expensive date that he has planned later in the evening. It is best in the beginning to keep the given circumstances fairly neutral, as in roommates or husband and wife at home. The second actor needs to come in with a purpose, and that purpose in turn will color the knock at the door.

However, whatever the purpose is, it is not directly referred to in the interaction. Once both actors are in the scene, it is all about responding off the other person. A typical scene might start off like this:

A: You look busy.
B: I look busy.
A: You look busy.
B: I am busy.
A: You are busy.
B: I am busy.
A: You are busy.
B: You're not helping.
A: I'm not helping.
B: You're not helping.
A: You're really stressed out.
B: I'm really stressed out.
A: You're really stressed out.
B: You're annoying me.

The scene creates the relationship, and because of the indirect nature of the encounter, real behavior is released. The use of the activity is a way of tricking the brain into not trying to control or shape the exchange. It is important early on for actors not to rush the exchange and to not leave the repetition too soon. It is easy for actors to fall into what seems like a natural conversation without waiting for a trigger for their impulse. "Don't do anything until something happens to make you do it" is a tenet that needs to be returned to again and again when doing Meisner work. In a large class, it is difficult to have everyone do the independent activity exercise, so it is may be necessary to select a few pairs to attempt it. When the exercise is done correctly, it provides both the viewers and the participants a concrete example of the absorbing nature of spontaneous moment-to-moment interaction.

In Meisner classes, the work is almost painstakingly slow and deliberate. This is because he was trying to disassemble the controlled self-image that actors tend to project through their acting in order to get back to an instinctive way of communicating even in a fixed text. The point is not that things like actions and objectives aren't a part of the equation. I may play a strong action that is inherent to my line, but it will be shaped by what I receive from the flesh-and-blood actor before me. If I am in a scene where I confess my vulnerabilities to a lover, and she responds "whatever," I could want to kill her. I also might be mildly perturbed or laugh. The idea in Meisner's approach is to let the actor's own impulses and not his analytical mind determine the result.

While working on these basic elements of the system can only give an introduction to Meisner's work, it does serve an important purpose. It provides students with the muscle memory of spontaneous interaction while at the same time providing tools to lock into their scene partner while being sensitive to their own impulses. The exercises are a source to return to again and again in order to establish the connection between scene partners. Furthermore, students need not end their experience of Meisner here. There is no doubt a wide spectrum of those who lay claim to being authentic teachers of Meisner's methods. However, students who want to further pursue his techniques have a unique advantage. Before he died, Meisner collaborated on a book that follows his teaching in an actual classroom and gives wonderfully precise insights into his approach and methods. *Sanford Meisner on Acting*, written with Dennis Longwell is unique among acting texts in its accessibility and efficacy. It also provides a candid portrait of one of the great figures in American theatre. Sanford Meisner not only understood deeply the importance of instinct in acting, he also found the means to awaken it in actors.

# PLATFORM 7: BERTOLT BRECHT

Bertolt Brecht is in many ways regarded by history as the anti-Stanislavski, a firewall against the inexorable movement toward naturalism.[65] He is mistakenly regarded as purely polemic, and for sure, he was never short of opinions. But he was a far more elusive and complex figure than is apparent at first glance. Consider these two quotes:

> This generation doesn't want to capture the theatre, audience and all, and perform good or merely contemporary plays in the same theatre and to the same audience; nor has it any chance of doing so; it has a duty and a chance to capture the theatre for a different audience. The works now being written are coming more and more to lead toward that great epic theatre which corresponds to the sociological situation; neither their content nor their form can be understood except by the minority that understands this. They are not going to satisfy the old aesthetics; they are going to destroy it.
>
> —*Bertolt Brecht, 1927*[66]

> From the first it has been the theatre's business to entertain people, as it also has of all the other arts. It is this business which always gives it its particular dignity; it needs no other passport than fun, but this it has got to have.
>
> —*Bertolt Brecht, 1948*[67]

While some twenty years passed between these statements, they are not so contradictory as would first seem. Brecht was always a showman and understood the nature of theatre as show business. His notion of epic theatre was to instruct and challenge an audience through entertainment. He did, in fact, rail at the theatrical tradition of Stanislavski as "the tasteless rehashing of empty visual or spiritual palliatives" and decried naturalism as a kind of narcotic that turns its audience into a "cowed, credulous, hypnotized mass."[68] Brecht saw theatre as a means of awakening society to self-knowledge and to an understanding of the human condition as a whole. Still, he knew it could never succeed at this lofty goal without being entertaining.

Brecht found his voice and his vision of epic theatre in his collaboration with the German director Erwin Piscator. Piscator, shaken by his experience as an infantryman in World War I, returned to confront the accepted conventions of popular theatre. He believed the burgeoning scientific age demanded a new form of art. He sought to do away with the single box set of naturalism and erase the fourth wall that formed a barrier between the actor and audience. He advocated a theatre in which actors spoke directly to the audience in a shared reality and opened up the playing areas to a shared space. In addition, he used film projection, mechanized sets, and written titles of scenes as a means of reinforcing the story in a nonillusionistic way.

This new style of epic theatre required a new type of acting. For both Brecht and Piscator, the ideal of embodying characters to produce an empathetic reaction in the audience was antithetical to the purpose of theatre. They both sought an actor who retained his human connection to society and who presented the character and action of the play without sentiment or emotional involvement. In short, they demanded storytellers. Piscator advocated objective acting, which requires the actor to separate from his creation in the same way as painters, musicians, and writers create a composition apart from their subjective selves. For Brecht, this same principle became the *alienation effect*.

Brecht coined the term *alienation effect* to the detriment of those who would try to unravel its meaning in the years that followed. His concept is not as confrontational as it may sound. As we have already learned, Brecht was a great proponent of entertainment in the theatre, so it is unlikely that his goal was to alienate the audience. Rather, he used the term to stress the importance of the actors not engaging the audience through empathy or emotional identification. The alienation that he is referring to is not between the actors and the audience, but between the actors and their characters. Brecht believed that the use of transformation in acting led to an emotional subjectivity that seduced the audience into a kind of hypnosis that blinded them to the larger implications of the story. All scenic and acting elements that led the audience into the illusion that they were watching actual events unfolding before them were, for Brecht, inherently false and destructive to the aim of theatre. He banished realistic sets and introduced elements such as spontaneous songs and written scene titles that were meant to jolt audiences back into the realization that they were, in fact, watching a play. His goal was to appeal to the audience's rational selves. He wanted them to understand not just a character's point of view of an event, but also the social forces that produced the event, the implications and ramifications of the event, and the other possibilities that existed within the event that were subject to the character's own choice. Brecht believed that by looking at human affairs with the detachment of a scientist, we could learn and see more than if we merely reacted emotionally in sympathy to a single character in a story. For Brecht, the larger story was far more important than any individual element, and in fact, the one piece of Stanislavski's system that he wholeheartedly embraced was the notion of the superobjective, the concept of an overarching theme that lent coherence to all the separate components.

While Brecht strongly advocated against a reliance on empathy, he did not believe in eliminating it altogether. Discussing the actor's use of empathy for the epic theatre, he wrote

> Yet in his efforts to reproduce particular characters and show their behavior he need not renounce the means of empathy entirely. He uses these means just as any normal person with no particular acting talent would use them if he wanted to portray someone else, i.e. show how he behaves. This showing of other people's behavior happens time and again in ordinary life (witnesses of an accident demonstrating to newcomers how the victim behaved, a facetious person imitating a friend's walk, etc.), without those involved making the least effort to subject their spectators to an illusion. At the same time they do feel their way into their characters' skins with a view to acquiring their characteristics."[69]

In other words, acting should be imitative and empathetic only to the degree that it serves an immediate purpose. The use of characterization and its inherent emotional aspects is not superfluous to his vision of theatre, but it is subsidiary to the larger goal of telling the story of the play. Characterization and empathy with the character's state of being are necessary only in that they serve the purpose of moving the story forward. He regarded the use of empathy as part of a process to be used in rehearsals and not as the ultimate goal of his actors. Indeed, he advocated much table work, critical analysis, and discussion so that the actors would be aware of the contradictions of their characters and the political and social context in which their characters' actions took place.

In his productions, Brecht often broke down individual moments into multiple layers of meanings. Costume, props, and pictorial groupings all contributed to representation of the complex and contradictory forces at work in his plays. Brecht's actors also employed the use of the *gestus*. The meaning of the term is even more elusive than the alienation effect. It is described by Carl Weber, a contemporary of Brecht as thus:

> The Gestus was to be mainly determined by the social position and history of a character, and Brecht instructed his actors to develop it by careful attention to all the contradictions to be discovered in the actions and verbal text of the role . . . this may sound quite abstract, but it was achieved during rehearsal in a most practical, even playful manner.[70]

While difficult to fully grasp, the term roughly means that the actor should not create a character subjectively. Instead, the notion of character must expand to encompass elements of class, social status, and history. Simply put, the composition of the character must include the context from which it emerged. This demanded that actors possess not just the ability to explore the subjective life of the character, but also the ability to observe, analyze, and be sensitive to the underlying social and political environment in which the character operates. While not exactly archetypical, the gestus was a means of creating character that resonated beyond the parameters of the immediate social situation. It was not, however, a purely intellectual concept. The gestus allowed actors at the Berliner Ensemble to create clearly delineated, moving, and comic characters. As pointed out earlier, for all his theoretical musings, Brecht believed that fundamentally theatre was about entertainment.

## EXERCISES: ENGAGING THE AUDIENCE

It is difficult to isolate techniques that are specifically Brechtian because so much of his methodology was in service to his own writing. However, we can utilize exercises that serve to redefine the actor's relationship to the audience in the manner Brecht had intended. The first of these is again taken from Keith Johnstone. It is an exercise called Beep, Beep. It may seem silly at first, but it is entertaining, and it does more to foster a direct connection to the spectators than any exercise I have found.

An actor enters and faces the class. All the spectators have their hands raised. The watching students are instructed that if the speaker fails to connect with them, they can gradually lower their arm. If it makes it to their lap they announce, "beep, beep." The standing student can use any simple text or even count to a hundred or recite the alphabet in a pinch. But, he must connect to each member or the watching audience as he talks. This simple act can be very intimidating to some actors. The opportunity to hide in a character in an imaginary world can provide actors with a sense of safety. When told to address an audience, their eyes instinctively float above our heads or make only rudimentary mechanical eye contact. If this happens, however, the arms maintain their steady progress downward. Only if they receive a genuine connection do the spectators raise their hands to the original position. As Johnstone points out, it is an impossible game to win "because the 'audience' has such a great desire to say, 'Beep, beep!' that they'll speed up!"[71] The best bet for the speaker is not to accelerate, but to stay calm and in control and methodically engage each spectator. As Johnstone points out, "The game breaks the polite social conditioning that teaches us not to make eye contact with strangers and as a result the audience feels recognized, engaged, and therefore warms to the speaker."

## OBJECTIFYING THE ACTION: THIRD PERSON PAST

Brecht devised a means for creating the alienation effect in rehearsal. He advocated using the following aids:

1. Transposition into the third person.
2. Transposition into the past.
3. Speaking the stage directions out loud.[72]

In other words, the actor narrates the action as well as performs it. After each line, the respective actor or actress states "he said" or "she said" along with whatever stage directions follow the action. This creates an intrinsic distance between the actor and the character and yet reinforces the notion that the actor is participating in a story that is being told. The use of the past tense also signals that the events are not happening in real time but have been considered within the context of the whole play by the actor who is now sharing it with the audience.

To put these techniques into practice, we return to the third neutral scene. Now as we remember, the given circumstances of the scene were devised by each set of actors. Those actors, therefore, understand the context and inherent meaning of the situation they have assigned to the words. Armed with this knowledge, they are to assign a title to the scene. It can be as simple as "A Scene about Temptation." The "scene about" form gives them a template to use, but it needn't be the only way of titling the scene. They can just name it as in "The Last Straw" or "A Love Scene." What is most important is that the title reflects a meaning that they have discovered through working on the scene.

After they have found a title, the actors proceed to add stage directions and add the third person past form. They may also add descriptive adverbs, as in "he muttered resentfully." "He said" and "she said" can be alternated with other descriptive verbs appropriate to what the actors have found in the playing, such as "he shouted," "she whispered," or "she questioned." The actors then rehearse the new form of the scene. Both actors speak the title either together or with each taking a part of the title. It is shared directly with the audience in accordance with the Beep, Beep exercise. The actors then play the scene with all the new narration. The object is to still play all the values established in the scene and maintain the action even through the narrative, without letting the concentration drop. The narrative is played with the same intention and is not spoken directly to the audience. This is what the new scene might look like.

## Neutral Scene 3: A Scene about Compassion

A: Please, he implored, holding up a picture of his missing wife.
B: I can't, he responded, not looking in his eyes.
A: Just try, he stressed.
B: I don't know, he said, weakening slightly.
A: Please, he repeated.
B: Can you? he started nervously.
A: Don't even, he asserted.
B: But, he implored.
A: No, he stressed.
B: You're mad, he realized.
A: Please, he said, softening slightly.
B: All right, he said reluctantly.
A: Ready? he asked.
B: You know I . . . he began, looking for sympathy.
A: What's that? he asked, businesslike.
B: Here, he said, handing him a file.
A: OK, he said, quietly putting it inside his jacket.
B: Great, he muttered, realizing what he'd just done.

In practice, this can be a maddening and frustrating exercise for certain actors, especially those who relish transforming into a character. But the fascinating thing is its effect on the audience. In most cases, the scenes do not diminish in their impact. Instead, the techniques serve as a framing device that focuses the audience's attention and forces them to consider the scene not as an actual event, but as an objective creation. It is almost like watching a three-dimensional novel. It is also unashamedly theatrical. The exercise is incredibly valuable in challenging the actors to find the meaning inherent in their text and to embrace the direct telling of the story to the audience. As Brecht had intended, the alienation effect does not produce coldness or passivity in the actor, but rather frees him from the need to convince the audience of the reality of the scene. Brecht allows the actor to realize the character and the story's impact on the audience by making it a conscious part of the work. What one finds in exploring the approach of Bertolt Brecht is what we have found in so many different forms of theatre. Once the audience recognizes the rules and parameters of how the story is being presented, they can still fully enlist in it on both a rational and a sympathetic level and give over to being entertained.

## PLATFORM 8: SCENE WORK

At long last, we have come to the point where the actors have amassed a range of tools and are ready to immerse themselves in scene work. By holding off this long, the students have had the chance to explore and to fine-tune a variety of approaches. At the same time, they are chomping at the bit to get working on characters and scenes.

The choice of scenes is very important. With younger actors, I find it is best to use ten-minute plays. These are available in anthologies such as *Take 10* and *Take 10 II* published by Vintage. The publishers of this book, Smith and Kraus, also publish ten-minute play anthologies. PlayGround, a San Francisco–based nonprofit group of which I am a member, regularly produces ten-minute plays in staged reading form on a variety of themes. They also publish anthologies annually, and there are several other books of short plays available as well. The advantage of the short play is that it is self-contained. All the given circumstances that one needs to uncover are there in the words that the actors will be saying. What is needed to fill it in and flesh it out is solely one's own imagination. The plays can very widely in terms of tone and style and I believe the instructor should cast them vary specifically to account for actors' strengths and what will be challenging to them.

In more advanced classes, I've found it best to select scenes from a particular period of theatre, such as American realism, or from a particular author such as Sam Shepard or Henrik Ibsen. Chekhov makes a wonderful choice, since he relies so much on multileveled human behavior and since he was such a formative influence for many of the theorists covered. The benefit of choosing scenes from a certain category or author is that it allows the work of the class to be collaborative and cumulative. Early on, they can and should share research on the period or the author, and as each actor's work progresses, it informs the work of others who are dealing with the same language and the same repertoire of behaviors.

Once the scenes are cast, the instructor should confer with each group to establish exactly how they want to work together. In the case of an advanced class, they will of course need to read and analyze the entire play in order to glean the given circumstances and the hierarchy of likes, dislikes, hopes, fears, and disappointments that inform each character. Over the course of the class, students have accumulated a range of specific approaches to the task at hand. They need to decide mutually how to put these pieces together. It is the job of the instructor to council, ask questions, and make suggestions. If a character discusses a memory, it is an opportunity to build an affective memory in order to make that moment sensorily alive. Do they want to work specifically on atmosphere? Do they want to build the physical life of the character through Chekhov's techniques? Do they want to score out the actions and objectives and mark the beats? Do they want to learn the scene by rote and use a preparation or simply work on repetitions with their partners as in Meisner? Do they want to use the Brecht work in order to focus on the story and meaning of the scene? Do they want to employ Johnstone's games to explore status or add emotional sounds and mantras to rehearse the scene? The actors needn't decide on their entire process up front. As the rehearsals progress, these approaches can help meet specific needs and overcome obstacles in bringing the scene to life.

After the initial consultation, I recommend dividing the class time into increments to rehearse each scene separately. At least in the early stages, it is better for the actors to work without the pressure of observation and to allow the rehearsals to be process oriented. If the scenes are from a single author or mode of theatre, they can be brought back and run together after a couple of weeks with merely note sessions as they move closer to final presentations. It is at this point that the work on each scene will start to inform the group as a whole. In the case of the ten-minute plays, I have found that it is best to work separately right up to final scene presentations so that the class can discover the plays for the first time in performance. Again, in both cases it is very important to return to a dialogue afterward in order to digest how the techniques were used, how successful the scenes were in terms of impacting the audience, and how specific tools might serve each individual actor in the future. Even though these scenes are what the work in class has been building to throughout, it needs to be stressed that it is all a process of developing and empowering each actor, and it is not about reaching for preconceived results. The scenes give the actors a means to concretize their process and build the muscle memory of actually using the techniques in the context of telling a story.

# PLATFORM 9: MONOLOGUE REHEARSAL AND PERFORMANCE

After the scene work, the actors will have a solid basis for understanding not only their own process and approach, but also the effect of their efforts on an audience. It is a necessary foundation, for as we noted earlier, monologue work has the potential to resurrect every bit of fear and self-consciousness and every bad habit that the scene work allowed them to overcome. If, however, an actor has been diligent in his search and found a piece that holds real meaning for him, it goes a long way toward overcoming these obstacles.

As we said earlier, a monologue is a snapshot from a larger story, but it should also be a story unto itself. We can take those three questions that an audience member asks and adapt them to the monologue form: Who is this person (and who are they talking to)? What is going on? Why do I care? We have to answer these questions if the monologue is to have an impact on the audience. In approaching a monologue from a storytelling point of view, the actor takes three steps. First, the actor recognizes what the impact of the monologue on the audience is intended to be. Are the spectators meant to laugh, to feel angry, to be outraged, or to be moved? The basis for recognizing this is the actor's own impressions when she first read the piece. Secondly, the actor looks for the structure that makes that impact possible. Any good monologue has an inherent structure. The structure, simply put, is what happens in the monologue. If it has an action structure, a change needs to take place. A realization is come to, a discovery made, a course of action chosen. The change can also be in the audience. A seemingly rational character can, in the course of the monologue, reveal him- or herself as highly neurotic or insane. This is a not unusual comic technique employed particularly effectively by Christopher Durang. The monologue can also be based on process, where a physical action is accomplished; or ritual, where spiritual and metaphysical overtones inform the piece as in a prayer; or ceremony, where the overt social structure of the event, such as a lawyer's opening statement or a funeral oration, determine the form. Classifying the category of the piece, however, is far less important than knowing how it works.

Having found the intended impact and recognized the structure, the actor then proceeds to the third step in the process—finding and using the tools to bring the piece to life. The reason for exploring the various techniques of this chapter is to have concrete means of taking the words off the page and making them personal and dynamic. As with the scenes, form follows function. Knowing what needs to happen helps the actors decide which tools to use. If the actor needs to speak directly to the audience, by all means, he should practice using the Beep, Beep game. But he should also personalize the relationship to the audience. The context of the monologue tells us if the audience is a group of supportive peers, authority figures that sit in judgment, or eager students wanting to have information imparted to them. The monologue tells the actor not just to talk to the audience, but how to talk to the audience. Likewise, if the actor is talking to another character he has to build the monologue as a scene. He has the opportunity to score in the other character's reactions to each line that he is saying and let those (unseen) reactions color how he progresses through the monologue. Even though that other person is not there, the actor's relationship to him or her both emotionally and sensorily has to be very specific. If the piece is a soliloquy, what is the character considering and what transpired to make the character speak at this specific moment? Shakespeare will often start a soliloquy with a question that the heart of the monologue considers before coming to a conclusion. As with most monologues, the first line needs to be triggered by a very specific stimulus. Grounding herself in the sensory and internal specifics of that moment allows the actor to be present and active from the moment she opens her mouth.

Most importantly when considering how to approach monologues, actors need to consciously avoid the impulse to show their work. The purpose of all these techniques is to allow the actor to be present and alive in his imagination and to communicate freely. The techniques have to be used in such a way that the work gets simpler and more essential, not more and more complex. The beauty of the monologue is that you can rehearse it anywhere—while jogging, while cooking, while in the shower. Monologues should be practiced over and over, always with the goal of simplifying. After performing the monologues, a dialogue is required. Again, the class provides a very necessary opportunity for students to realize the impact they have made through the work and to learn what adjustments need to be made to further enhance that impact.

As with any technique, the goal is for the work to disappear so that the playing is enjoyable and seemingly effortless. The actors need to use these techniques consciously to solve specific problems so that they will become ingrained and unconscious later on. Experienced actors don't necessarily apply these methods like a chef following a recipe in a cookbook. Over time, they have nurtured a sensitivity to texts and an empathy to situations that allows them to recognize unconsciously what needs to be done to bring plays to life. That is what we are all aiming for. It is the synthesis of technique and personal creativity that truly makes us artists. It is not alchemy. There is no great mystery to acting as an art form. It simply demands hard work and imagination and an awareness of the foundations that have been laid down by others. Just like physics, literature, or music, acting must draw on the accumulated wisdom of those who came before us.

> Bernard of Chartres used to say that we are like dwarfs on the shoulders of giants, so that we can see more than they, and things at a greater distance, not by virtue of a ny sharpness on sight on our part, or any physical distinction, but because we are carried high and raised up by their giant size.
>
> —*John of Salisbury,* Metalogicon *1159*[73]

# 💧8

# OTHER VOICES

hile the techniques of the previous chapter reveal a range of methods that evolved over several years in locations thousands of miles apart, they are still but a fraction of the many approaches to performance being taught and practiced in the world today. Even as you read this, there are individuals exploring and expanding the boundaries of theatrical language. To offer a comprehensive listing of the many teachers, theorists, and practitioners who have influenced or continue to influence the art form would be an impossible task. However, in the interest of providing other avenues for investigation and a broader context, here is a brief listing of some of the other seminal figures and approaches in the development of the modern theatre along with sources for further exploration.

## STELLA ADLER (1901–1992)

Not only was Stella Adler a witness to the events that changed American acting, she was a major force for change. A renowned member of the Off Broadway and Yiddish theatre communities, she became a leading actress with the Group Theatre. It was her sessions with the aging Stanislavski that led to a reappraisal of their working methods and the split with Lee Strasberg. After she left the Group, she was a major figure in actor training at the New School for Social Research, her own Stella Adler Studio, and noted graduate programs such as the Yale School of Drama. Her interpretation of Stanislavski's system incorporated paraphrasing, improvisation, and personalization to bring the emotional reality of the plays' situations to life for the individual actor. She stressed a strict adherence to the given circumstances and emphasized the use of imagination to justify each physical action onstage.[1]

## F. M. ALEXANDER (1869–1955)

Matthias Alexander, an actor in Australia at the turn of the last century, was a specialist in Shakespearean oratory, until his chronic laryngitis disabled him. Rather than succumbing to the condition, Alexander methodically analyzed its causes and effects. The result of his efforts produced a technique that is practiced worldwide and featured in many acting programs. The Alexander technique is a kinesthetic discipline of freeing neck tension and reducing compression on the spine. The resulting lengthening opens the channels of the articulators and resonators permitting freedom from undue tension and strain. His methods expanded to encourage the efficient and dynamic use of the body across a range of activities and physical functions.[2]

## ANTONIN ARTAUD (1896–1948)

An actor, director, and writer, Antonin Artaud is best known as a theorist. Living in Paris during the Surrealist period of the twenties, he rebelled at the traditions of French theater. Artaud battled madness for much of his adult life and was in and out of sanitariums. This perhaps influenced his concept of a nonnarrative theatre that could transform its audience through primitive and violent expressions of unconscious fears and longings. He envisioned a combination of elements of oriental theatre and modern technology as a means to produce awe and terror in the spectator and at once awaken him to his dangerous primitive self and liberate himself from it. "Theatre of Cruelty" was for him a sacred initiation that aspired to a transcendent, metaphysical truth. While he only staged a single production (*The Cenci*, an adaptation of works by Shelley and Stendahl), his theories have influenced generations of artists that followed, and his book, *The Theatre and Its Double*, has had a lasting effect on dramatic theory.[3]

## AUGUSTO BOAL (1931– )

Raised in Brazil and educated in New York City, Boal returned to his native country and began his theatrical experiments. Boal sought to change the Aristotilean-based theatre that he saw as a monologue of preordained outcomes into a dialogue that involved the audience in the action. He created the concept of the "spect-actor" and invited audience members onstage to help resolve issues and discover outcomes to his drama. He sought to bring social justice to disadvantaged communities through theatre and, as a result of his efforts, was imprisoned, tortured, and exiled by the Brazilian government. In exile, he wrote *Theatre of the Oppressed*, which became a manifesto for his theories of theatre. Boal is perhaps most influential for the workshops he has taught throughout the world and for the many games and exercises he has developed that work to break down the barriers between actor and audience and impact social change. These are detailed in his second book, *Games for Actors and Non-Actors*.[4]

## ANNE BOGART (1951– )

As a director with a background in dance and performance studies, Anne Bogart has created a unique synthesis of movement and theatre through her development of viewpoints. Originally created by choreographer Mary Overlie as means of characterizing and shaping movement, the viewpoints have been adapted by Bogart as a system for training and generating theatrical work. They create a physical architecture of performance that can enhance or contrast with the relationships and words of a text. From the original six components, she has developed at present nine: spatial relationship, shape, kinesthetic response, repetition, gesture, architecture, tempo, duration, and topography. Ensemble members of the Saratoga International Theatre Institute, the company she cofounded with Tadashi Suzuki, are fluent in the application and integration of these components, and they use them as a point of entry to a text. In addition to her extensive directing work, Bogart has also served as artistic director at Trinity Repertory Theatre in Providence, Rhode Island. She has taught widely at universities and training programs throughout the country, in addition to the specific viewpoints training at SITI. She is the author of *The Viewpoints Book*.[5]

# PETER BROOK (1925 – )

Peter Brook was directing major productions at the Royal Shakespeare Company in his early twenties. He became one of the most innovative and experimental figures in English theatre, as witnessed by his famous staging of Peter Weiss's *Marat/Sade*, based on the theories of Antonin Artaud. In the seventies, he founded the Center of Theatre Research in Paris and assembled a company of performers from all over the globe. He has sought to use this company to create universal stories that cross the boundaries of culture and nationality. His 1985 production of *The Mahabharata* is one of the most world-renowned productions of the last several decades. It told an epic story from ancient Hindu Sanskrit and lasted over nine hours. His career has represented an evolution toward a simple, direct means of sharing stories with audiences that represent an unconscious collective experience. Peter Brook has also directed noted film adaptations of *The Lord of the Flies* and *King Lear* and is well known as a writer on theatrical forms. His books include *The Open Door, The Shifting Point,* and his widely influential text *The Empty Space*.[6]

# ROBERT BRUSTEIN (1927– )

As founder of the Yale Repertory Theatre and dean of its drama school and founder of the American Repertory Theatre and its conservatory training program at Harvard, Robert Brustein has played as big a role as anyone in the growth of regional theatre and conservatory training in America. He is also a professor at Harvard, a distinguished critic and author, a director, and a playwright. Not shy about his opinions, Brustein has given voice to the potentials and pitfalls of American theatre and invited debate about the avant garde, nontraditional casting, and professionalism in the theatre. He has been an astute chronicler of theatre for over forty years. Among his many books and collections are *Making Scenes, The Theatre of Revolt,* and *Who Needs Theatre?*[7]

# JACQUES COPEAU (1879–1949)

Based on what he saw as a theatre critic in Paris, Jacques Copeau resolved to create a new theatre by rediscovering the impulses and instincts that had created the French classics in the first place. Copeau's company secreted themselves in farmhouse in the French countryside to deurbanize their acting mannerisms and strip away the vestiges of artifice through intensive physical and vocal exercises. The company that emerged, the Théâtre du Vieux-Colombier, became a national institution. An exhausting taskmaster, Copeau produced a large repertory of classic and modern plays and eventually started his own training academy.

After ten years of national and international acclaim, he closed his theatre to concentrate on the training of actors. Once again he took his troupe to a farmhouse, this time in Burgundy, to train and work on process. Due to financial conditions, the company failed, but a core remained. This core formed les Copiaus, a new company based on the model of the original commedia dell'arte companies, and toured the small towns of Burgundy to much renown. In both his training and production, Copeau sought an aesthetic essence, devoid of artifice and infused with a sense of play. He employed mask work and highly disciplined physical and vocal exercises. Copeau is valued for his vision as well as his influence. The famous director Louis Jouvet was a close collaborator. Another collaborator, Michel St. Denis, achieved international recognition for directing and went on to found the Old Vic Theatre School in England and the acting division of Juilliard in New York City. Jacques Lecoq, who formed his own famous school of physical acting, was also a member of his company.[8]

## RICHARD FOREMAN (1937– )

As the founder and artistic director of the Ontological-Hysterical Theater in New York and a director of international acclaim, Richard Foreman has been a mainstay of New York's Off Broadway scene for over thirty years. He has written, designed, and directed over fifty of his own plays, in addition to directing acclaimed productions of Brecht, Molière, and Gertrude Stein, among others. Taking his cue from Bertolt Brecht, Foreman seeks not to provoke empathy in the audience, but rather to disorient them and challenge their perceptions in order to awaken them to the fragmentation of communication in the modern world. Drawing from both poetry and film, Foreman creates a series of tableaux and vignettes built obtusely around a given theme and without any conventional narrative structure. He has incorporated multimedia into his more recent productions and also has also directed videos and film. He is the recipient of numerous grants, and awards, including nine Obies. His published works include *Richard Foreman: Plays and Manifestos* and *Reverberation Machines: The Later Plays and Essays.*[9]

## JERZY GROTOWSKI (1933–1999)

Starting out his theatrical life as an actor in Poland, Grotowski traveled to Moscow to study directing in the tradition of the Russian greats, Stanislavski, Meyerhold, and Vakhtangov. In 1956, he returned to Poland and immediately began to tackle an eclectic range of texts, from French absurdism to Indian folktales to contemporary Polish authors. His evolving Laboratory Theatre achieved prominence in Poland and attracted acclaim at International Festivals.

As he evolved as an artist, he became increasingly preoccupied with process. Grotowski was fascinated by the ritual nature and universal themes of theatre, and he believed in stripping theatre to its most essential elements. His concept of a poor theatre relied on the direct relationship of the actors to the spectators, and he designed an architecture that blurred the divide between the two. He similarly believed that acting needed to be more than just an accumulation of tricks and devices, and his process for training actors was to strip away the defenses and social masks that prevented a pure expression of their inner life. Grotowski believed in a sacred theatre whose unrefined expression of man's deepest fears and taboos could help to heal and renew society, and he promoted a stringent physical and vocal training regimen to meet the demands of his vision.

As Peter Brook said of Grotowski in his influential book, *The Empty Space*, "In Grotowski's terminology, the actor allows a role to 'penetrate' him; at first he is an obstacle to it, but by constant work he acquires technical mastery over his physical and psychic means by which he can allow the barriers to drop. 'Auto-penetration' by the role is related to exposure: the actor does not hesitate to show himself exactly as he is, for he realizes that the secret of the role demands his opening himself up, disclosing his own secrets. So that the act of performance is an act of sacrifice, of sacrificing what most men prefer to hide—this sacrifice is his gift to the spectator."[10]

Grotowski was forced to emigrate to the United States. He set up his research at UC Irvine in California and later went to Pontedera, Italy, where he worked until his death. As he matured, he became more and concerned with theatre as anthropology and explored the nature of ritual across cultures and societies. His book *Toward a Poor Theatre* is one of the most influential texts in modern theatre.[11]

# UTA HAGEN (1919-2004)

Born in Germany, Uta Hagen grew up in Wisconsin and went on to become one of the preeminent actresses of her generation. She was the original Martha in Edward Albee's *Who's Afraid of Virginia Woolf?*, a role for which she received one of three Tony Awards. She is perhaps best known for her teaching. Together with her husband, Herbert Berghoff, she was a fixture at the HB Studio in New York where she was a major influence in the development of American acting. Her two books on the subject, *Respect for Acting* and *A Challenge for the Actor,* are seminal texts. They give testament to her incredibly detailed and insightful process of scoring a role and using analysis, experience, and imagination to enter into the moment-to-moment life of a character.[12]

# RUDOLF LABAN (1879-1958)

Born into an established military family in Austro-Hungary in 1879, Rudolf Laban turned away from his background and propelled himself into the world of movement and choreography. Having studied architecture as a young man in Paris, Laban become fascinated with the architecture of the human body in space. In Germany between the two world wars, he had a prolific career in dance, having established two companies, a main school, several amateur dance "choirs," as well as publishing articles and choreographing and performing new works. Forced to emigrate to Britain with the rise of the Nazi party, he began a new career, researching the efficiency of movement for industry. This in turn led to his devising a systemized vocabulary for movement and choreography. While he was an artistic pioneer in the world of modern dance, he is best remembered for his establishment of a highly specific system for notating choreography and movement. His work on capturing and describing physical behavior has had a large impact on training actors in a range of movement dynamics. The following description provided by Keith Johnstone is a thumbnail version of Laban's much more extensive system.[13]

| Weight | Space | Time |
|--------|-------|------|
| Heavy | Direct | Sudden |
| Light | Indirect | Sustained |

Selecting one quality from each column gives you eight choices:

- Heavy-Direct-Sudden describes punching.
- Heavy-Direct-Sustained describes pushing.
- Heavy-Indirect-Sudden describes slashing.
- Heavy-Indirect-Sustained describes wringing, as in wringing out a cloth
- Light-Indirect-Sustained describes stroking.
- Light-Direct-Sudden describes dabbing.
- Light-Direct-Sustained describes smoothing.

# VSEVOLOD MEYERHOLD (1874–1940)

As a young actor with the Moscow Art Theatre, Meyerhold played Treplev in Stanislavski's most famous production, Anton Chekhov's *The Seagull*. Mirroring his character's search for "new forms of art," he became a prominent director and moved away from Stanislavski's early naturalism to productions that were ever more abstract and nonrealistic. In his relatively short life, he directed over 290 productions, including experiments with commedia dell'arte, symbolism, and constructivism. He developed his own very specific training method for actors: biomechanics. This highly demanding physical system was designed to forge a connection between body and mind so that actors develop kinesthetic and spatial awareness in addition to their emotional and analytical skills. Because Meyerhold was executed by the Soviet regime in 1940, much of his writing and details of his work were purged from public records, but changes within the Russian political system have led to a reevaluation of this gifted and influential artist.[14]

# VIOLA SPOLIN (1906–1994)

A renowned educator, director, and actress, Viola Spolin began developing her system of theater games under the auspices of Neva Boyd. Boyd was an innovative teacher and social worker who sought out games and nontraditional methods to engage and affect inner-city youth in Chicago. As she progressed as a teacher and director, Spolin built on the techniques she had learned from Boyd to construct games as techniques for freeing actors from self-consciousness and to restore a sense of playfulness in their work. She used these techniques to train actors of all ages and together with her son, Paul Sills, established what would be the home for improvisation in America, The Second City Company of Chicago. She is the author of five books on theater games, most famously *Improvisation for the Theater*, which contains over two hundred of the games she developed.[15]

# TADASHI SUZUKI (1939– )

Seeking to find a new theatrical vocabulary that could be at once kinetic and eloquent even in stillness, Tadashi Suzuki looked to the Japanese traditions of Noh and Kabuki to translate their virtues to a modern context. He saw the modes of contemporary performance as overly codified and sought to reconnect to the "animal-energy" of the past. The method he created involves a firm connection with the ground that activates the lower body and energizes the breath. He alternates strong movement with stillness and seeks to transform the body to an intense almost abstract instrument of communication. These techniques form a dynamic language that contrasts with the texts of Western plays he interprets in his productions. He originally developed his methods with his Suzuki Company in Toga, Japan, but he has been widely influential in America, teaching at SITI, the company he cofounded with Anne Bogart. He is also the author of many books on acting, *The Way of Acting* being his most well known.[16]

# YEVGENY VAKHTANGOV
## (1883–1922)

One of a trio of Stanislavski's protégés, Yevgeny Vakhtangov was a brilliant and gifted director. Unlike Meyerhold and Michael Chekhov, however, Vakhtangov did not depart from Stanislavski's system and used and adapted it to bring even more experimental productions thrillingly to life. It was through his work with Vakhtangov that Chekhov first arrived at the concept of the psychological gesture. Vakhtangov used aspects of the system, such as justification, to bring personal truth to his actors even in the most heightened and abstract productions. He used several nonnaturalistic elements such as dance, masks, music, and design in his noted productions such as *Turandot* and *The Dybbuk*. One can only wonder at how far he could have extended the uses and evolution of Stanislavski's system, as he died tragically of cancer at age thirty-nine.[17]

# COMMEDIA DELL'ARTE

Though its origins remain largely speculative, commedia dell'arte was the first professional theatre in Europe. It was an immensely popular form that existed from the early sixteenth century until its decline in the eighteenth century. Although companies had to tour towns and cities throughout Europe, its greatest practitioners were embraced by the royal courts of France and throughout the continent. Commedia is often thought of as improvisatory, but this is only partially true. Companies would rehearse a season's worth of scenarios before a tour, and each actor kept journals of *lazzi*, comic business, and excerpts of classical poetry to use in performance. Each actor would be assigned a type that they would repeat throughout a season in different scenarios. These included *zannis*, or clowns, such as Arlecchino; Capitano, a braggart soldier; and Pantalone, a foolish old man. All the characters, with the exception of the young lovers, wore masks. Commedia also featured female performers long before the English stage. The style was fast and presentational, and while often comic, the companies were also capable of high drama. The immediacy of emotional states, swift reversals, and physicality of expression are hallmarks of commedia that have extended through the work of Molière to vaudeville and situation comedy and even to modern interpretations by companies such as the Actor's Gang in Los Angeles and The New Criminals in Chicago.[18]

## THE LIVING THEATRE

Judith Malina was a student of Piscator's at the New School and teamed up with the painter Julian Beck to form the Living Theatre in 1947. Originally, the company focused on choreographed stagings of abstract and poetical works from authors such as Gertrude Stein and Pirandello. The company evolved toward a more direct involvement with the audience in productions such as Jack Gelbers' *The Connection*, which focused on the world of drug addicts and Kenneth Brown's *The Brig*, which became the company's unifying cry against the forces of authority. From the sixties forward, the Living Theatre became a communal-based company dedicated to a political vision of anarchy and rejection of authority. Artistically, they created actual live ritual-based events in opposition to the rehearsed performances of the commercial theatre. Strongly influenced by Artaud and Brecht, they sought to break down the barriers between audience and actor and through confrontation and participation explore universal themes of violence and repression.[19] An early member of the company, Joseph Chaikin, left to form the Open Theatre. His vision was less political than that of the Living Theatre, but similarly focused on a collaborative process that investigated universal themes such as death (*Terminal*, 1970) and notions of paradise (*The Serpent*, 1969). An acclaimed director, he was widely respected as an interpreter of Beckett and was a longtime collaborator with playwrights Jean-Claude van Itallie and Sam Shepard. He is author of *The Presence of the Actor*, a journal and compendium of his process.

# 9

# TELLING
# CLASSICAL STORIES

One of the greatest challenges for both actors and directors is how to approach material from a classical repertory. Indeed, it has been one of the great conundrums for many of the practitioners we have discussed. Whether the plays are from ancient Greece or from the golden ages of France, England, or Spain, they place special demands on those who would share them with a modern audience. It is important to remember when confronting a classical text that the play will have many inherent cultural, religious, and political references that will not be readily accessible either to us or to our audience. Instead of seeking to explain them or to translate them into a modern naturalistic context, we need to aspire to the scope and breadth of the original story and seek through our efforts to inhabit the world of the play. To do this, we need to lay a foundation.

For the purposes of narrowing a very broad category, this chapters focuses on the plays of William Shakespeare. While certainly there is a world of distance both in terms of idiom and cultural tradition between England's theatrical renaissance and the others, there is much in the approach to language and verse that is universal. I once had a teacher tell me that Shakespeare was the Olympics of acting. I think of him more specifically as the decathlon of acting because he demands an actor to be in top condition and to do so many different things well.

In conversation with actors of all ages, I have found some consistency in their impressions. What they tend to find intimidating is speaking verse, the archaic nature of some of the language, and inhabiting situations and characters that are by nature heightened and unfamiliar. What is exciting is the fullness of the worlds that Shakespeare created, the richness of the language, and the fact that despite the antiquated aspect of some of the language, much of Shakespeare's comedic and dramatic writing from four hundred years ago remains exceptionally vital today. Overcoming the obstacles and living inside the words of Shakespeare is a subject for exhaustive exploration. However, in the interest of brevity, I will limit the range of my investigation to some essentials.

## KNOW WHAT YOU'RE SAYING

It seems rather obvious, but you would be surprised at how many experienced actors play only the gist of their understanding of some words without fully investigating the meaning. A reasonably good edition of any of the plays will offer editor's notes on meaning and usage, and there are many good lexicons and glossaries that can provide detailed definitions. But that is just the beginning of the work on language. We must realize that we are a visual culture. Visual media inundates us, and it informs our perception and communication. English society of Shakespeare's day was an aural culture. They could process a great deal more language and imagery at a faster rate than we can today. Shakespeare used language to paint visual pictures and to give concrete imagery to abstract notions. What modern storytellers do with sets, lighting, editing, and camera angles, Shakespeare did with suggestion. "Let us, ciphers to this great accompt, on your imaginary forces work,"[1] says the Chorus in *Henry V*, inviting the audience to forgo a realistic depiction for the sake of participation in a shared world of their own imaginations.

Many of the references in Shakespeare are specific allusions to elements of Elizabethan and Jacobean society that hold no meaning for an audience today. An actor can spin his wheels trying to clarify a word or phrase and not come close. However, if he understands the reference and how and why it is specifically used, he can still use the words as they were originally intended. A modern audience will on a good day pick up only a percentage of the vocabulary that confronts them in a Shakespeare play. What they will perceive, however, is the relationships that connect characters, the relative status of those inhabiting the world, and what is going on between them all. They will, that is, if the actors let the words inform them. "Suit the action to the word, the word to the action,"[2] says Hamlet to the players. If the actors heed his advice, the action will be clarified for the audience by the words, and the words will reinforce the actions. Even with all of Shakespeare's rich language, the audience should be able to follow the story, even if it were viewed behind a soundproof pane of glass, based on the action alone.

The gifted voice teacher and director Kristin Linklater devised an exercise called "dropping in," where she isolates words from a Shakespeare speech that an actor is working on and mulls them over with the actor as he sits comfortably with eyes closed.[3] The word *death,* for example, can lead to questions such as: Is death a hooded skeleton with a scythe? Have you ever felt like dying? What does a dead body look like? The actor repeats the word after each question, all the while breathing deeply. The idea is to restore the personal connection we have with images. If we are experiencing the images as we speak them, the audience may not perceive all the individual meanings of the words, but they will sense our experience of them. Shakespeare used words not only for their literal meaning, but for their sounds and senses as well. He used alliteration, onomatopoeia, and antithesis all for the sake of activating words and making them live for an audience. The challenge and the benefit of Shakespeare is that he uses language to convey the experience of the characters so that if we are alive in the language we are immediately connected to the audience. In a room filled with tuning forks, they will all resonate when a single one is sounded. Just so, the audience responds unconsciously when the words are truly activated by the actors.

# IAMBIC PENTAMETER

While Shakespeare was renowned for his poetry, much of the text of his plays, specifically the comedies, is in prose. He generally uses verse in the heightened speech of characters of the upper echelon of society. To look at verse as merely a more formalized manner of communication, however, would be a gross simplification. The verse Shakespeare employs is flexible and expressive and not something foreign to assay. To speak in verse is not innately hard. The sentence you just read, in fact, is verse. So was that one. I point this out as a means to illustrate that iambic pentameter is designed to mirror natural speech.

Iambic simply means the stress is on the second syllable, as in "I *am.*" Pentameter refers to the fact that in a line of verse there are five (penta) stressed syllables, as well as five unstressed syllables. This form was adapted as a naturalized version of the Greek and Latin verse line, and it led to an explosion of poetic expression in the Elizabethan age. The verse line mirrors the beating of a heart and has a natural forward momentum.

When the verse line is broken by what is known as a trochee, it means a word shifts from the second syllable emphasis to a first syllable emphasis. These typically appear in the first word of a line of verse, but they can also appear in the middle of a line. When you come across one, you can generally assume that it is a word that demands emphasis. It creates a jarring effect to have the regular rhythm suddenly interrupted. So the word that forms the trochee will tend to be important for the meaning.

There is also the feminine ending, which means that there is an extra unstressed syllable at the end of a line, as in "To be or not to be that is the question." This typically means that the thought is not completed and follows to the next line, as it does in *Hamlet.* The line "Whether 'tis nobler" picks up the extra unstressed syllable with a stressed trochee. An alexandrine is a line with an extra two syllables, and while it somewhat rare in Shakespeare, it is the preferred structure of the famous French poets Jean Racine and Pierre Corneille.

This all seems rather academic, but it is far from it. The verse actually assists memorization and comprehension. It's like a road map into the play. Knowing the iambic structure tells you how words are pronounced. A verse line that becomes erratic can also be an indicator of a character's emotional state. In his early plays, Shakespeare was very regular and scrupulous in observing the verse form. In his later plays, he explored distorting and stretching the bounds of the form to conform to the increasing scope of what he was seeking to express.

## SPEAK UP

This in no way refers to volume. Instead, it refers to inflection. One of an actor's most important tools in approaching Shakespeare is the use of rising inflection. If the actor strictly adheres to the verse line, it starts to assume the cadence of a Dr. Seuss book. However, if the actor learns to follow the continuing logic of thought through the lines of verse by using a rising inflection, it starts to resemble human conversation. Read a section of verse from Shakespeare and try taking a deep breath after each line. As you will see, the rhythm overwhelms the meaning, and it starts to lose its sense. But if we connect the lines that continue a thought and breathe only where the thought is completed, the verse shakes off its sing-song quality and starts to convey meaning.

This again is not something unnatural to modern speakers. We use a rising inflection whenever we ask a question, as in "What are you doing?" So-called valley girls  from southern California, infamously portrayed in films such as *Legally Blonde*, tend to use rising inflections at the end of both statements and questions. For example, imagine the following said with rising inflections: "How's it going?" "I love that dress." "You want to go to the mall?" "We're all going in Jen's car. You can come too." Such vocal mannerisms are a clear distortion. But becoming aware of inflection and learning how to use rising inflection is invaluable.

The more accustomed an actor becomes to using rising inflections, the more she can extend meaning through large sections of verse. The rising inflection also informs the audience to keep listening, whereas the continuous use of a downward inflection gives them the impression that the thought is finished and the speech is ended. Try reading a speech with a downward inflection at the end of each line, and you will most likely find it starts to take on a monotonous quality that makes it seem much longer than it actually is. As with the use of the trochee, when a downward inflection is used, it will stand out as a point of emphasis. Using rising inflections in a natural way is one of the best means of depoetizing Shakespeare and making long passages of verse seem fluid and expressive of both thought and feeling.

## NOT ALL WORDS ARE CREATED EQUAL

Shakespeare uses a rich and varied vocabulary of images and verbs. It can be daunting to assay some of the larger passages. But it is far less intimidating if you get rid of half the words. What I mean by that is to focus on the words that carry the meaning of the text. I had a teacher once who told me to analyze passages of Shakespeare as if I needed to send a telegram. Now I know that is a hopelessly outmoded analogy, so I'll invite a new one. Imagine that you need to text-message the essential sense of a passage to someone. What are the crucial words that do the heavy lifting in creating meaning? Look at the following passage. What stays and what goes?

> I left ~~no~~ ring ~~with her~~. ~~What~~ means ~~this~~ lady?
> Fortune forbid ~~my~~ outside ~~have not~~ charmed ~~her~~.
> ~~She~~ made good view ~~of me~~: ~~indeed~~ so much
> ~~That~~ me thought ~~her~~ eyes ~~had~~ lost ~~her~~ tongue,
> ~~For she did~~ speak ~~in~~ starts distractedly.
> ~~She~~ loves ~~me~~ sure: ~~the~~ cunning ~~of her~~ passion
> Invites ~~me in this~~ churlish messenger.
> None ~~of my~~ lord's ring? ~~Why~~ he sent ~~her none~~.
> I ~~am the~~ man. ~~If~~ it be so, ~~as~~ 'tis,
> Poor lady, ~~she were~~ better love ~~a~~ dream.
> —*Twelfth Night* II, ii, 17–26[4]

Now let me say that while there are certain rules to this, a lot of it is subjective. It's all about what carries the meaning. Why did I strike out some words and underline others? Here are the reasons:

- Personal pronouns unless they are part of a direct comparison, as in "You thought this, but I thought that," must go. They carry too much weight and trap the speaker in a needless emphasis. (An exception is where the pronoun is clearly the point of the line as in line 9.)
- Small words such as *in, the, to, of, at, a, for* are merely linking and don't merit emphasis.
- Generally, when a word is repeated within a couple of lines, (see *none* in line 8), the repetition is not emphasized.
- Negatives such as *no, not,* and *nor* are so strong to the listener's ear that they don't demand emphasis to elaborate meaning.
- Nouns and the adjectives that modify them are almost always underlined.
- Verbs are the active components of the speech and are therefore kept and underlined.
- Words that are neither crossed out nor underlined serve a purpose in conveying meaning but without the emphasis of those that are underlined.

By analyzing the text this way, we give ourselves a means to activate the verse both for ourselves and for the audience. What can seem like a long and impenetrable section of verse becomes active and clear. Emphasis is crucial to conveying meaning.

Consider the following sentence: I went to the game with John. It seems like a fairly straightforward statement. However, if we imagine it in a dialogue as an answer to specific questions or statements, we can see how emphasizing different words conveys different meanings. For example:

"I heard John went to the game with some friends."
"*I* went to the game with John." (No, it was I who went to the game with John.)

"So John gave you a lift home from the game?"
"I went *to* the game with John." (No, he took me there.)

"Are you going to go to the game with John?"
"I *went* to the game with John." (No, it already happened.)

"Did you and John go to a game?"
"I went to *the* game with John." (It wasn't just "a" game, it was important.)

"Did you go to a concert with John?
"I went to the *game* with John." (It wasn't a concert, you daft fool, it was a game.)

"Did you meet John at the game?"
"I went to the game *with* John." (We went together.)

"Did you go to the game with Phil?"
"I went to the game with *John*." (Not Phil, John.)


As you can see, even a relatively simple statement conveys different meanings based on the words we choose to emphasize. It is therefore essential in approaching Shakespeare that we know which words to emphasize to convey the intended meaning. The context tells us what those words are.


# RHETORIC

In looking for clues that provide the context for which words are emphasized, we might as well use the system that Shakespeare used when he wrote. Originally devised by the Sophists in ancient Greece as a system of persuasion in public speaking, rhetoric was further codified by the Romans and survived the fall of the empire to be widely disseminated and taught in the type of English grammar school that Shakespeare likely attended. The tropes, schemes, and figures of rhetoric were as well known to the Elizabethan schoolboy as multiplication tables are to schoolchildren today.

Brian Vickers has done an excellent study of the uses of these different linguistic effects in Shakespeare, and I cite some of his samples here as a means of entry into the structure of the form.[5]

*Anaphora*, the most common of all rhetorical figures, repeats a word at the beginning or a sequence of clauses or sentences;

> Then curs'd she Richard, then curs'd she Buckingham,
> Then curs'd she Hastings      (*Richard III*, III, iii, 18–9)

That example also used *parison*, in which within adjacent clauses or sentences word corresponds to word (either repeating the same word—curs'd—or else grouping noun with noun, adjective with adjective, etc.). A more exact use of *parison*, putting great ironic stress on the final word, is this:

> Was ever woman in this humour woo'd?
> Was ever woman in this humour won?
>                     (*Richard III*, I, ii, 227–8)

Both these examples increase the effect of symmetry by using *isocolon*, which gives exactly the same length to corresponding clauses, as again the Duchess of York's catalogue of a family's distress:

> She for an Edward weeps, and so do I:
> I for a Clarence weep, so doth not she.
> These babes for Clarence weep, and so do I:
> I for an Edward weep, so do not they.
>                     (*Richard III*, II, ii 82–5)

. . . *Ploce* is one of the most used figures of stress (especially in this play), repeating a word within the same clause or line:

> . . . themselves the conquerors
>
> Make war upon themselves—brother to brother,
> Blood to blood, self against self.   (*Richard III*, II, iv, 61–3)

. . . *Epanalepsis* repeats the same word at the beginning and end of the same lie, as with "themselves" in the example for *ploce* above, or again with Richmond's reflections on Hope:

> Kings it makes gods, and meaner creatures kings.
>                     (*Richard III*, V, ii, 24)

A related figure is *anadiplosis*, which gives the same word the last position in one clause and first (or near the first) in the clause following. It rightly expresses causation, as in Richard's impatience:

Come, I have learn'd that fearful commenting
Is leaden servitor to dull delay;
Delay leads impotent and snail-pac'd beggary
(*Richard III*, IV, iii, 51–3)

If *anadiplosis* is carried through three or more clauses, it becomes a figure known in Greek as *climax* ("a ladder"; in Latin gradation), and is again suitably used for causation in Richard's despair:

My conscience hath a thousand several tongues,
And every tongue brings in a several tale,
And every tale condemns me for a villain.
(*Richard III*, V, iii, 193–5)

Now this is but a sampling of what Vickers cites, which is in turn but a fraction of the total figures that were known to the Elizabethans. Do you have to know the difference between a *ploce* and an *isocolon* to act Shakespeare? No, of course not. But we must realize that Shakespeare was not just winging it. Knowing that he was employing very specific techniques designed to produce eloquence allows us to use those techniques to *be* eloquent. We may not be as familiar with rhetoric as the Elizabethans were, but we can recognize when and how it is being used. This technique literally tells you where the emphasis goes. Combining it with the crossing out and underlining image technique, along with the investment in vocabulary, permits the actor to access all the functions of the language in order to carry meaning across to the audience.

# VARIETY IS THE SPICE OF LIFE

Now that we have a playbook for approaching Shakespeare, what can we do to enact it? As Americans we tend toward flat, unstressed speech. With the exception of some regional dialects, ours is not a musical tongue. This is ironic, for many experts maintain that American speech, specifically certain dialects along the Eastern Seaboard, is actually closer to the spoken English of Shakespeare's day than the standard speech commonly used in modern England.[6] All the more reason for American actors not to "Britishize" their speech when assaying Shakespeare. But where Americans will come up short is in the musical aspect of speech. This is where we need to make consciously technical adjustments at first, so that they may become innate as we move forward.

In looking at Vickers' final figure from the previous section, climax, we are faced with a challenge. Something described as a "ladder" obviously has an intrinsic movement to it. When we are faced with these rhetorical structures that use repetitive images, they need either to build up or to build down.

How do we accomplish such a build? We have another set of tools: the four P's—Power, Pitch, and Pace. Used together or apart, they create variety in speech. In order to practice, an actor needs a bit of verse that is neutral, in as much as the actor will not be attempting to interpret it. Instead, she will consciously apply each of the tools at first separately, then in combination. To do this, one needs to visualize a staircase. With each progressing line, the actor takes a single step up either in pitch or in power, the level of volume, or in pace. She should also practice reversing the build, wherein with each line the volume decreases, the pitch lowers and/or the pace slows down.

So far I have only mentioned three P's. There is also a wild card to throw in—Pause. It should be used judiciously because it can unnaturally distort a verse line and quite often if Shakespeare desires a pause at a given moment, he builds one into the verse. Nonetheless, it is another means of creating variety by arresting the ear of the listener and focusing the audience on what is to come. One may feel like a ham actor while practicing these exercises out loud, and that's OK. The conscious rehearsal of the exercises along with the assiduous practice of the warm-up described in the chapter 7 can develop a strength and flexibility to the voice that will become natural and unself-conscious in a relatively short span of time.

# BREATH AND FORM

So far everything in this chapter has been about language techniques. That is appropriate. How many times do musicians practice
scales before they can undertake a concerto? However, the marriage
of external technique to internal technique is what makes classical
works come alive. Here are some approaches that focus more on the
internal aspects of Shakespeare;[7]

- The breath you take is as important as the line you speak. If
  the breathing is emotional, the articulation will be meaningful. When you have the two together, you have a reasoned
  being. Breathe with the intention of the action, not with the
  desire to speak well. Don't take unnecessary breaths.

- Every time you use a simile, you must find a reason for it.
  Words are only the public expression of a personal experience. When you use an image, you must look for the thought
  or impulse that needs concrete expression, and then find it as
  if for the first time. If you make the discovery before the audience, it will seem vital and real. If you merely recite it, it will
  sound like poetry in quotation marks.

- Beware of playing one tone or emotional note throughout a
  speech. All the speeches are journeys that begin at one place
  and end somewhere else. Find all the colors along the way.

- Do not move unless absolutely necessary. As Hamlet says to
  the players, "Do not saw the air too much with your hand,
  thus; but use all gently, for in the very torrent, tempest, and
  (as I may say) whirlwind of you passion, you must acquire
  and beget a temperance that may give it smoothness."[8] It is
  tempting to physicalize the language because it feels more active, but it will not clarify it.

- Shakespeare wrote fast, the plays were rehearsed fast, and
  they were performed fast. He employed an episodic structure
  that allowed for a constant forward momentum. Don't play
  for speed, but play with momentum.

- Use irony. Shakespeare's characters' self-awareness is one of
  the qualities that sets him apart in the annals of literature.

Not only are they aware, they comment on themselves ironically, directly to the audience. Always look for irony.
- Believe it or not, you can get away with doing much less than
you think. The beauty of Shakespeare is that he has done so
much of the work for you.

# A BRIEF MODEL FOR A SHAKESPEARE CURRICULUM

## SONNETS

The sonnets are a collection of 154 poems written over several years of
Shakespeare's life.[9] They represent a diverse wealth of themes, tones,
and intentions. Many Shakespeare scholars have tried to piece out a
narrative through-line to the entire body of work and speculate on the
identity of characters contained in them such as "the dark lady" and
"the fair youth." Such considerations are outside of our scope. What we
are seeking to do is to use the sonnets as a entrée into Shakespeare. The
sonnets are almost entirely uniform in their structure. They are in
iambic pentameter and follow a scheme where rhyming words match
the following letters *abab cdcd efef gg*, illustrated here:

| | |
|---|---|
| My mistress' eyes are nothing like the sun; | a |
| Coral is far more red than her lips' red; | b |
| If snow be white, why then her breasts are dun; | a |
| If hairs be wires, black wires grow on her head. | b |
| I have seen roses damask'd, red and white, | c |
| But no such roses see I in her cheeks; | d |
| And in some perfumes is there more delight | c |
| Than in the breath that from my mistress reeks. | d |
| I love to hear her speak, yet well I know | e |
| That music hath a far more pleasing sound; | f |
| I grant I never saw a goddess go; | e |
| My mistress, when she walks, treads on the ground: | f |
| And yet, by heaven, I think my love as rare | g |
| As any she belied with false compare. | g |

—*Sonnet 130*

Now the sonnets pursue many different themes. In several, the speaker is imploring someone to procreate and produce likenesses of his or her beauty. Others follow themes of betrayal, longing, disappointment, and, of course, love. The first lines tend to establish the premise. The body of the sonnet investigates the theme through imagery, and the final lines either reverse the argument or reach a conclusion. Every actor in a class should choose one that specifically appeals to him. Once a sonnet is chosen, each actor needs to do the scansion and imaging work from above.

After the analytical work is done, the first task is to identify the tone of the sonnet. Is it ironic and humorous, as in number 130 above, or is it a painful confession or an adamant self-defense? Once the tone is found, one must discover who is being addressed and why. The answers will comprise the given circumstances, such as they are. The specifics are pure speculation, but one can discern a sense of what is going on. The next step is to form a relationship to the language through the dropping-in exercise cited earlier. In addition to the one-on-one image work, I have also had an entire class lie in a relaxed position on the floor with their eyes closed as I "drop in" images compiled from all of their chosen sonnets. Once again, the purpose is to establish a personal relationship to the words and images.

The final step is to personalize the sonnet and who is being addressed. Actors need to answer the question "Why am I saying this now?" The sonnet needs to have an impetus, an imperative reason for being expressed. The task is to relate the situation of the sonnet to the actor's own experience. The personalization and specification of the circumstances allow the actor to have an intention so that the sonnet becomes active and not merely recitative. Finally, the class does the sonnets for one another. However, the performance, such as it is, consists of the actors seated in a circle of chairs speaking the words simply. There is no effort to "perform" them. This first stage is about experiencing the language in the present tense so that meaning, intention, and imagery are conveyed simultaneously.

# PROLOGUES AND CHORUS

The next step in the curriculum is to assay a particular feature that appears in a relatively small percentage of the plays, the use of a prologue or chorus. The useful aspect of these speeches is that they are verse, they are full of images, and they are purely narrative. In other words, they are telling stories. Their function is to set the stage and provide the necessary background for the larger story of the play or to link a play's separate episodes. In some instances, they are character neutral as in the Chorus of *Henry V* or the Prologue of *Romeo and Juliet*. Other examples, such as Gower in *Pericles*, Time in *The Winter's Tale*, or Rumour in *Henry IV*, part 2, are narrators who assume the role of characters. In these instances, however, characters are essentially emblematic, their primary qualities as characters serve as a function of their role as storyteller. That is one of the benefits of working on prologues. It allows the actor to invest in a rich image-laden narrative without the encumbrance of having to construct a complex character. It also allows the actor to confront one of the distinctive features of Shakespearean acting; direct address.

Shakespeare uses direct address often in plays not merely as a means of narration, but also to engage the audience and pull them into the story. Unfamiliar as it is to a twenty-first-century actor, being able to comfortably communicate directly with an audience is a crucial aspect of playing Shakespeare.

To get acquainted with direct address, we return to Keith Johnstone's Beep, Beep exercise.[10] Actors start off with a simple rhyme or the alphabet and move to doing their prologue while the spectators "beep, beep." As a reminder, each member of the audience starts with one arm raised and starts lowering it slowly during the monologue until she feels the speaker has connected with her personally, at which point she returns the arm to its original position and begins lowering again. This connection has to be registered by the audience member and is more than mere eye contact. If no connection is made and the arm makes it all the way down to the spectator's lap, she says "beep, beep." The exercise forces the actors to relate directly to the audience. But what is the nature of that relationship?

Another Johnstone exercise, known as Low Status Trick Presentation,[11] gives us a foundation for our interactions with an audience. The premise is simple. Two actors alternately approach the audience, perform a difficult trick, accept the audience's applause, bow, and leave. The catch is that there is no "trick." In lieu of an actual trick, actors say the word *trick*, or improvise some ridiculously simple bit of business, but behave as if it is immensely difficult. It is an exercise in consciously raising the status of the audience. Johnstone advises, "Run on with small steps to demonstrate your eagerness, and be so happy that it's obvious that you'd never dream of challenging their superiority. See them and bow, see them and say, "Trick," see them and bow again, and see them before leaving."[12] Seeing and connecting directly with the audience ". . . allows you to give us friendship signals, and to be yet more pumped up with inner delight each time you realize how wonderful we are."[13] The audience in turn must applaud enthusiastically at the efforts displayed. As the exercise proceeds, this will be easier because the more the performers buy into the situation, the more fun they are to watch. This technique of lowering the actor's status and raising the audience's is used very specifically in a number of prologues including in *Henry V*: "O Pardon, gentles all, the flat unraised spirits that hath dared on this unworthy scaffold to bring forth so great an object."[14] In all the prologues and speeches, there is a single action: to make the audience excited about what they are going to see. The basic good nature displayed in the exercise can be adjusted with different qualities to accommodate the demands of the different speeches.

Once again, the actors must proceed through the analysis of the text to clarify and personalize the images. They work on the Beep, Beep and "trick" exercises to explore their relationship with the audience. As they work on them, they can start to bring in some of the acting work from chapter 7, such as atmospheres and qualities. But the primary focus of the prologues is to tell the story directly to the audience.

# MONOLOGUES

The next step is to tackle monologues, which allows us to move into the realm of character. Now a monologue is clearly any extended bit of text spoken by one character. It may be prose or verse. It can be a soliloquy, where the character is alone onstage, or it can be a speech to another character that is part of a larger scene. As with prologues, characters can step outside the action of the play and talk directly to the audience. Perhaps more so than with contemporary monologues, it is important for the actor to find a piece that truly excites him because of the extent of the analysis and preparation that a Shakespearean monologue requires. Not only does the actor have to do the text work already cited, he then needs to ground himself in the play's given circumstances, including the social and political context of the period portrayed as well as Shakespeare's own age. Finally, the actor needs to do all the acting work one would do for any monologue. The monologue work is important for a number of reasons, not the least of which is that it is hard to get a job acting in any of Shakespeare's plays without having an effective monologue.

In approaching the monologue, it is important that we bear in mind the overall structure. It is analogous to a single instrumental solo in an entire symphony. We have to understand the relationship between the two. Shakespeare employed an episodic structure, meaning he freely jumped between different times and locales and focused on different characters in the overall story. This allowed the action to be flowing and continuous. Each scene and monologue serves the function of moving the story forward. So the actor must ask, What purpose does this monologue serve? In other words, what does the audience know after the monologue that it didn't know before? Some monologues, such as the Porter's from *Macbeth*, are set comic pieces that serve to shift the tone and focus and work as bridges for the central narrative. Others, such as many of Hamlet's soliloquies, are considerations of a dilemma or are contemplations that move toward resolution. They allow us to get the sense of a character's state of being in the midst of the flow of action. Knowing how a monologue fits into the overall framework of the play shapes the work on the monologue itself. We can then look to the verse and choice of images as clues to the character's state of mind and their actions. We can use the tools we have already established to see how the rhetorical devices function and to create variety to match the forms of expression. Finally, we can use all of our acting tools to create the character behind the words. We can use the Chekhov work to change our physical selves and to correspond to the specific atmospheres of the given circumstances. We have to ask, What has just occurred to make me say these words now? We can then use Meisner or Strasberg to ground ourselves in the emotional preparation that forms the undercurrent to the speech. Certainly, we can use Johnstone's exercises when we are talking directly to the audience. Even in these instances the actor's choices have to be specified. The actor needs to shape the audience she is talking to based on the given circumstances. Am I talking to a jury of my peers to seek approval for my actions? Or am I challenging them in a boastful way to appreciate the machinations I have set in place, as does Richard III? Even a soliloquy can use the audience as a sounding board to clarify a character's internal impulses outside the unfolding action of the play.

Even though we are separating the speech from the body of the play, we need to draw from the play to simplify our work. Since rehearsals were short and Shakespeare knew his company well, he put all the needed information in the words. We need to construct the full world of the play in our minds so that the monologue then becomes a necessary expression of a specific moment of the overall action. There is still plenty of room for interpretation. For the true challenge of the monologue is to be alive and have the true experience of the character as we speak the lines. Two different actors doing the same analysis and considering the same given circumstances of a given monologue can have vastly different takes on it based on their own personalities and points of view and neither will be a wrong interpretation. That is what has made Shakespeare a constant challenge for actors to return to in the almost four hundred years since his death.

# SCENES

You may notice that I have inverted the structure of the "In Class" curriculum, which has monologues come last. That is because the analysis of structure and language needs to become second nature for the actors before engaging in the moment-to-moment work on scenes between multiple characters. In many ways, Shakespeare scenes mirror contemporary scenes in the use of given circumstances, actions, and objectives. However, in Shakespeare the means are primarily verbal. Shakespeare uses wit, puns, rhetoric, and bawdry all as actions between characters. Indeed, in scene work, actors need to be aware that not only can a character take over an iambic verse line from another character, he or she can echo the same rhetorical devices and turn the imagery against the speaker. That is why all the early analytical and text work needs to be done as a team. From the start, actors need to see how the language functions to heighten the values and intentions of the scene.

Once the actors have done the text analysis and understand the language, the acting work begins to take over. This is where most of the techniques covered can come in to play. We just need the means to know how to apply them. Since we know that Shakespeare uses an episodic structure and that every scene and monologue serves as a function of the larger story, we just need to ask what that function is. What has to transpire in order to impact the audience in the intended way? We can even put it in Brechtian terms and give the scene a title. Once we know what has to happen, we can look at it closer and see how we can increase the tensions and create complexity instead of just fulfilling the surface demands.

For example, let us consider the famous scene in *Richard III*, in which Richard seduces Lady Anne in the presence of her husband's corpse whom Richard has murdered.[15] Those are the facts. However, if we see Richard's advances only for the political advantage he is seeking, the scene may be audacious and malevolent, but it will be lacking in a dimension of tension. Just as he convinces Anne, we must buy into the possibility, however remote, that Richard is somehow truly expressing vulnerabilities and emotions that we never thought he possessed. As he convinces Anne, he must also convince us. While in the whole of the play, Richard is certainly a villain, in these moments he can't appear to be one. In turn, this allows Anne to act the truth of the situation and fight all the way until her final acquiescence. This then makes the "Was ever woman in this humour woo'd" line truly chilling instead of merely comically ironic.

As Brecht pointed out, in every situation there is another possible outcome and we need to see that possibility in the choice that the characters make. By taking away the predetermined aspect, we make the comedy more human and therefore funnier and the tragedy less inevitable and therefore more painful. Shakespeare's characters always need to be at risk. It is a part of what makes them alive in each moment. In order to create that moment-to-moment life, we can start to use our acting techniques. The atmospheres, qualities, and psychological gesture of Chekhov scream to be used in Shakespeare. Objectives and physical actions, beats, and given circumstances, so crucial in Stanislavski's approach to naturalism, are equally important here. Meisner's techniques are useful in emphasizing the listening and observation, two crucial aspects of the actor's work on Shakespeare that tend to be the first things to be abandoned. From Strasberg, we can take relaxation and emotional memory, which have already undoubtedly informed our investigation and personalization of images. Obviously, status transactions can be part of the work, and I have even introduced Keith Johnstone's emotional sounds and mantras into Shakespeare scenes to wonderful effect. Which techniques the actors use is a matter of preference and emphasis. The goal is to build a technical and analytic foundation. The acting methods then allow the scene to take off. In any Shakespeare class, I recommend building a final presentation drawing from both the scene and monologue work. The sharing of the worlds that the actors have inhabited and invested in is the last crucial aspect of the work they have been doing.

Now this represents only a piece of the work that one can do when approaching Shakespeare. What we haven't touched on is the investigation of the worlds of both the play and of Shakespeare's era.

Seeing paintings, understanding the history, and realizing the belief structures of a different time can further excite the imagination of the actor. This is work that can be done for all plays in the classical canon. It is in fact the purpose and obligation of approaching classical texts. Our job as storytellers is to mine the rich landscape of a play and bring back tangible, playable values that can impact and affect our modern audience. They can do so because we as actors have done the investigative work that has let the plays' meanings permeate us. We are translators. In a sense, our work is both creative and anthropological. It does require a different skill set, however. As this chapter has pointed out, there are specific means at our disposal to analyze and inhabit the language of a different time and place. We must use them. But the act of taking words from four hundred to two thousand years ago, the symbols of an antique culture, and bringing them to life theatrically is nothing short of an amazing accomplishment.

# 🌿 10

# TELLING NEW STORIES

I f Shakespeare is the Olympics of acting, then working on new scripts is the high-wire act. I say this firstly because every choice an actor makes in rehearsal of a new text can affect the final form of the play and secondly because the impact of the play remains a mystery until its first time in front of an audience. Having said that, it is important to point out that every great work of drama was an untested new play at one point. Plays such as *The Seagull* and *Hedda Gabler* were, in fact, accounted failures in their initial productions. While there is a heightened sense of risk in undertaking new scripts, there is also a commensurate reward for the actors in the process.

Understanding that there are many different forms and structures involved in playwriting, we can rightly surmise that every playwright has a particular process. We need to realize that the writing of the play tends to be a particularly isolating exercise. Writers have heard the voices of the characters in their heads thousands of times and have sweated over the specific phrasing of each line. It is no wonder that they can be a little sensitive about the liberties an actor may take with their words. It is therefore best to be as scrupulous as possible in observing the exactness of the phrasing and punctuation of the text. The actor's job is to use her faculties to inhabit the specific language the playwright has devised. Based on the actor's best efforts to do so, the playwright can then make adjustments to the script that will clarify and elaborate his vision. That is one of the most exciting aspects of working on new texts, but it can also be extremely challenging. Getting rewrites minutes before going in front of an audience is not an uncommon thing. It is therefore best to stay flexible and remember that whatever best serves the play best serves the actors.

Having a playwright present in rehearsals makes it tempting to simply ask him all the questions you have about your character or the play. This can be dangerous, however. Many directors like to act as the sole liaison between playwright and actors. Many, in fact, prefer working with dead playwrights. It can be a difficult collaboration. A playwright has labored alone to put a vision on the page, and now that a production nears, oft times he will chafe at any departures from the image of the production that existed in his mind. Similarly, playwrights may not possess the specific skills or vocabulary to help actors to achieve the results they desire. The director is responsible for the story's impact on the audience, and she must be allowed to shape the production and guide the performances. The lines of division need to be respected. It is, nonetheless, an incredible opportunity to be able to collaborate with a living writer.

In many ways the work on a new play mirrors the work on a play from an established repertoire. We still need to look at the structure and see how it is intended to impact an audience. We need to understand the tone as well. Is it satirical? Is it realistic, or does it exude a particular style in its dialogue? Stanislavski advocated looking for the play's superobjective, meaning a predominant theme or the element that inspired its writing. Playwrights are generally loath to explain their inspiration. Often however, with the director's blessing, playwrights are happy to discuss the world of the play and the specific research they have done. It is another trap to try to look for the playwright's approval during rehearsal. The writer may or may not be enjoying the specific choices an actor is making. But most likely he is thinking of something else. That miserable look on his face is most likely in reference to a rewrite he wishes he had done or a line that isn't working.

Every process is different. Sometimes plays are workshopped and their characters, structure, and plot undergo radical changes. Other times a play will differ very little on opening night from the version of the first rehearsal. How much a script changes is not a barometer for the actors to use to gauge their success or failure. Sometimes plays get better with rewrites, and sometimes not. While actors are not expected to be dramaturges or critics, they do have a role in this process. Having worked on a character from a subjective point of view, the actor can elucidate and articulate the interior mechanisms of the character. In this context, changes can certainly be discussed with the director, but knowing how is important. A phrase such as "It just doesn't feel right" or "I liked the other line better" is less useful than "Losing that line undermines my objective for the scene" or "We've lost some necessary information about where she's coming from." Having stated a point of view, it is then necessary to step back and let the other creative players mull over their options. Even when a change occurs that an actor is not particularly happy about, such as losing a favorite line or speech, ultimately the job of the actor is to commit to the words that remain.

In some instances, the work is almost completely collaborative. I worked at the Magic Theatre in San Francisco on a new piece by the Joe Goode Performance group that was a joint creation between three dancers of his group and three actors, of which I was one.[1] We did several gestural and physical improvisations as well as character and writing exercises. From this, Joe would compile and write an unfolding narrative. It was one of the most unique and exciting acting experiences of my career. The benefit of this type of highly participatory process is that it gives the actor a deeper stake in the piece and allows him to see the evolution of his work in immediate relation to the audience. It is another facet of the direct role of actor as storyteller and harkens back to an age when actors weren't merely hired at the tail end of a creative process, but were active participants in it.

Whatever the particular process involved, the nature of the work on a new script has some essential benefits. One does not have to burden oneself with notions of how other actors have interpreted a role. In this way the dialogue can seem immediate and spontaneous because it is not "preowned." It is also immensely satisfying when a writer shapes new elements to a script based on an actor's work in rehearsal. The inverse is also true. It is as much a testament to an actor's talent when a playwright excises sections because they have become redundant based on how much of the story the actor is able to tell through her action and behavior alone.

Perhaps the most important element of working on new texts is that word *new*. Because it is so, an evolving work of drama has the potential to redefine the relationship of the actors to the audience and explore untried and untested avenues of expression. Drama is constantly changing to reflect the changing face of its society and to be an active part of that evolution is an incredibly demanding and exciting part of being an actor.

# 11

# TELLING STORIES:
# WHERE WE ARE NOW

For the entertainment industry today, these are the best of times and the worst of times. The increasing polarization of our society is mirrored by a polarization of the business that entertains us. It is the age of the megablockbuster. Every major movie studio produces and promotes tent-pole films, hugely budgeted movies that are released on thousands of screens in the hopes of offsetting their underperforming films and those failures that go straight to the DVD store shelves. Box office numbers that reveal the winners and losers in this competition are printed in the paper like baseball box scores. Meanwhile, independent filmmakers, after struggling to make their films, struggle to get into film festivals in the hopes that they can get picked up by a distributor, and then struggle to get attention in a crowded marketplace of releases.

Television producers spend millions of dollars on pilots, which face daunting competition to be picked up by television networks. Most of these new shows are cancelled, and even the ones that survive lose money. Producers are willing to lose this money in the hopes of getting enough episodes produced to sell the show into lucrative syndication and finally reap a huge return. Both television and film producers are adjusting their product to accommodate delivery on demand to computers, cell phones, and personal video players, so that entertainment becomes less communal and more focused on the individual consumer.

In theatre, Broadway and touring ticket prices routinely top $100. A hit Broadway show with ancillary revenues from touring productions, can gross hundreds of millions of dollars. Off Broadway and regional companies inevitably plan their seasons with an eye to potentially moving productions to Broadway and hitting pay dirt. But as in the movie and television businesses, most of these endeavors fail. While one successful Broadway play can keep a company in the black for years, the steadily increasing costs of production force companies to produce shows with smaller sets, smaller casts, and less development.

The increased stakes in all these fields has led to an increase in corporate producing and partnership in order to lessen the burden of risk. In the riskiest business in the world, everyone is looking for the means to avert risk. This typically means giving an audience what the producers presume it wants. Sequels along with adaptations from popular books, TV shows, and even video games populate the multiplexes. Actors are cast in accordance with their "Q" rating, a system that quantifies their popularity with the public and, hopefully, the box office returns that popularity can guarantee. Broadway musical budgets have exploded, and special effects shots have increased severalfold in the average studio movie, as film and stage productions strive to become more and more spectacular. All of this is in service to finding the elusive magic elixir of what the public will actually pay to see.

Meanwhile, that public is overwhelmed. We are faced with many choices and limited time. Modern man is becoming numb to the onslaught of options and the ever-increasing stimulation of modern media. Faced with a multitude of home entertainment options, it is understandable that the potential audience wants a guarantee. If a modern couple has to pay a babysitter, pay for a dinner out, pay for tickets, and then invest two to three hours of their attention and concentration on something, they are right to want to know that they will enjoy it. Still, art can never provide that guarantee. This environment is especially deadly for theatre. An unenjoyed DVD can be returned half watched. A channel can be changed. Even a disappointing movie can be walked out of, and in the modern multiplex, a potentially more enjoyable movie walked into. Yet theatre kills a little of its audience every time it disappoints.

Theatre has a particular relationship to its audience. Stanislavski said of the theatre audience; "If you want to learn to appreciate what you get from the public, let me suggest that you give a performance to a completely empty hall. Would you care to do that? No! Because to act without a public is like singing in a place without resonance. To play to a large and sympathetic audience is like singing in a room with perfect acoustics. The audience constitutes the spiritual acoustics for us. They give back what they receive from us as living, human emotions."[1]

There is something unique in theatre that has survived even to this day. To sit in a theatre, be it large or small, is to commune with not only the actors onstage but the other members of the audience that surround you. Actors and audience are both witnesses and participants in a shared experience. It is different from performance to performance, and it is a living event. A movie or a television show can be moving, but it will not be affected by your presence. It is ultimately a thing. But like a sporting event or a concert, live theatre requires and thrives on the energy and focus of a living audience. Good theatre rewards that investment with an experience that is reflected in Stanislavski's words and will indeed live in each particular audience member's memory. But theatre that disappoints does so because it demands so much of the spectator and then falls so far short of its potential to affect him. Thus disillusioned, the spectator, having committed the time, money, and effort demanded by the experience, questions his willingness to engage in the process again. Its very relevance is called into question. For theatre, it is always a matter of one step forward and two steps back.

At many points in its history, theatre has been pronounced a dying form. Many of its golden periods were followed by barren periods where it became irrelevant or died out completely. Our media age presents a new challenge, and once again the future of theatre is in doubt. But the survival and vitality of theatre does not require a wholesale reimagining of its form or content. Theatre has always been an elastic and adaptive form, and its diversity of approaches and expressions is one of its greatest strengths. Instead, we, as actors, need to rediscover our relationship to our audience. What Brecht, Stanislavski, Shakespeare, and all the great figures of the theatre realized was that theatre's success, both aesthetically and commercially, depends on its ability to speak specifically to the society of which it is a part.

Theatre is fulfilling a tradition as old as society itself. For as long as we have existed together, we have needed the means to investigate ourselves and our role in the world we inhabit. Storytelling is necessary to the health of any civilization. The stories that define us are not mere diversions and distractions. They reflect the longings and questions, the doubts and fears, and the wonder and delight that form the connective tissue of a society. A robust and vibrant theatre is the reflection of a society strong enough to look unreservedly at itself. This is what Shakespeare meant when he had Hamlet describe the purpose of acting as " . . . to hold, as 'twere, the mirror up to nature, to show virtue her own feature, scorn her own image, and the very age and body of the time his form and pressure."[2] The fact that theatre is a communal form means that those participating in an event are doing so as part of a community. That will always be what sets theatre apart from its burgeoning competition in the media age. Theatre demands physical and spiritual proximity. To be present at a play means to be willing to have an experience in public as part of the public. The more we isolate ourselves through digital media, the more we lose a defining part of what we are; ourselves as a society.

Theatre is not a cure for all that ails modern man and woman. But its purpose from its inception has been to engage its society and investigate issues and meanings that are by nature collective. That is our starting point, and it represents a tremendous responsibility and a tremendous opportunity for the theatrical community. We have to know how to do our jobs in service to the stories we are telling. The story is always the organizing principle. It defines our relationship to the audience as well as the work we will do. It reveals how we are to tell the story, and why it is important to tell it at this moment in time. Once again, story is not plot. It is all the levels of meaning that coalesce into an aesthetic effect on the audience. If we know how to look at the story, it will disclose the mechanisms and the methods that we can use to impact our audience.

The telling comprises all the work that we as actors have done or will do to share the story. It is our relationship to the text as well as our relationship to the audience. Actors are the crucial direct link that makes a story live and breathe for an audience. Our task is to accumulate methods and tools that allow us to articulate at the highest level the values and significances we have divined from our contact with the story. That is why acting does not require some magical "it" that only special individuals possess. Clearly there is such a thing as innate talent and certainly there are qualities like humor, or charm, or sex appeal that make performers appealing. But great acting is not just showing off. It is taking a collection of people on a journey night after night. To do that, one must believe that the journey is worth taking and that those people deserve to go on it with you. That essential relationship has been the defining force in theatre from its roots in ancient Greece to the present day. It is just as possible in a storefront theater in a small town in the middle of nowhere as in a massive Broadway house.

Theatre is most definitely in a precarious position today. But it is not merely economic and technological factors that are threatening its existence. We need to get better at this. For the longest time, actors have existed in a kind of tower of Babel, where everyone has different vocabularies, different approaches, and believes fundamentally different things about the job at hand. We are isolated and forced to compete with one another. Young actors emerge every year from acting programs without knowing the history or context of the very things they have been studying. It is not surprising that for many, the first thing to abandon them is the pleasure they initially took in acting.

It is for this reason that we need to rediscover what is thrilling and dynamic about the theatrical event. The techniques explored in this book are reflective of artists who fought to maintain their passion and love for the craft of acting throughout their lives. We cannot afford to retreat behind any particular ideology. As we have seen in the previous pages, these methods are not so very much in opposition to each other. They have all been tested by the crucible of time and all have much to offer the actor who is willing to explore them. They represent an invitation. We have to find our courage, lose our egos, and be willing to take chances. We must be adaptive and aware of the audience to whom we are telling stories and open to the tools that support us and free our imaginations. Above all, we must never forget the pleasure we first took in sharing stories with each other.

# Notes

## 2 How Did We Get Here?

1 Constantin Stanislavski, *An Actor Prepares* (New York: Theatre Arts Books, 1942), 43–45.
2 Constantin Stanislavski, *My Life in Art* (New York: Theatre Arts Books, 1948), 298.
3 Stella Adler, *The Technique of Acting* (New York: Bantam Books, 1988), 120.
4 Sanford Meisner and Dennis Longwell, *Sanford Meisner on Acting* (New York: Vintage, 1987), 34.
5 Michael Chekhov, *To the Actor* (New York: Perennial Library, 1985), 63–84.
6 John Willet, *Brecht on Theatre* (New York: Hill and Wang, 1964), 91–99.
7 Eric Bentley, "Stanislavski and Brecht" from *Stanislavski and America: "The Method" and Its Influence on the American Theatre*, Erika Munk, ed. (Greenwich, CT: Fawcett Premier, 1967), 117.

## 3 A New Paradigm Arises

1 Fresh Air from WHYY interview with Ian McKellen, December 19, 2003.
2 Sharon M. Carnicke, "Stanislavsky's System: Pathways for the Actor" from *Twentieth Century Actor Training*, Alison Hodge, ed. (New York: Routledge, 2000), 17.

## 4 How It Works

1 Workshop at the Playwright's Foundation, San Francisco, Calif., Nov. 2005.

## 5   Storytelling and Character

1 David Mamet, *True and False* (New York: Vintage Books 1997), 9.
2 Michael Chekhov, *To the Actor* (New York: Perennial Library, 1985), 85.
3 Uta Hagen, *A Challenge for the Actor* (New York: Scribner, 1991), 55.
4 *Hamlet*, III, i, 73.

## 6   The Structure of the Story

1 This section is based in large part on notes from the lectures of Professor Leon Katz, Yale Drama School 1983–1984.
2 Richard Feynman, *What Do You Care What Other People Think?* (New York: W. W. Norton & Co., 1988), 11.

## 7   In Class

1 Keith Johnstone, *Impro for Storytellers* (New York: Routledge, 1999), 131.
2 Freely adapted from warm-ups taught by Linklater voice teachers Zoe Alexander, Virginia Ness, and Timothy Douglas, as well as speech teachers Robert Palmer of the Royal Academy of Dramatic Art and Deborah Hecht of the Yale School of Drama with reference to the following texts: Kristin Linklater, *Freeing the Natural Voice* (New York: Drama Book Publishers, 1976); Linklater, *Freeing Shakespeare's Voice* (New York: TCG, 1992); Edith Skinner, *Speak with Distinction* (New York: Applause, 1990).
3 Lewis Carroll, *Alice's Adventures in Wonderland and Through the Looking Glass* (New York: Everyman's Library, Children's Classics, 1992), 220.
4 This section is comprised of direct quotes and notes recorded from two workshops with Keith Johnstone hosted by Bay Area TheatreSports, San Francisco, on August 16, 2006, and on August 14, 2004. It also refers to material found in Johnstone's books: *Impro* and *Impro for Storytellers*.
5 Ibid.
6 Ibid.
7 Johnstone, *Impro for Storytellers*, 130–31.
8 Ibid., 156–60.
9 Ibid., 34–36.
10 Ibid., 134–42.
11 Ibid., 368.

12 I was told by an actor friend, Rod Gnapp, that this was a Johnstone game, but it is most likely an adaptation, as I have not found it anywhere in his writing. As Johnstone himself says on the subject, "Creating an improvisation game from thin air is almost impossible (the best you can do is to adapt existing games). This is because games are an expression of theory." Ibid., 130.

13 Ibid., 221–22.

14 Another adaptation of Johnstone.

15 Johnstone, *Impro for Storytellers*, 223–26.

16 Ibid., 228.

17 Ibid., 163–66.

18 Ibid., 156, 188, and adaptations.

19 Ibid., 366, and adaptation of a "Viewpoints" game. See www.siti.org/, Jan. 2007.

20 Ibid., 171–177.

21 Ibid., 177–178.

22 Ibid., 202–4.

23 Ibid., 310–14, 185–86.

24 Ibid., 233–36.

25 Ibid., 178–80.

26 Ibid., 364.

27 Ibid., 316–17.

28 Ibid., 211, 268–70, 270–74.

29 Ibid., 211.

30 The primary texts for this section are: Stanislavski, *An Actor Prepares*; Toby Cole, ed., *Acting: A Handbook of the Stanislavski System* (New York: Crown, 1979); Stanislavski, *Building a Character* (New York: Theatre Arts Books, 1975); Stanislavski, *Creating a Role* (New York: Theatre Arts Books, 1978); Stanislavski, *My Life in Art*; Carnicke, "Stanislavski's System" from *Twentieth Century Actor Training*.

31 Dacher Keltner, Psych 156, fall 2006, UC Berkeley Podcast, 2006, UC Regents; Paul Ekman, *Emotions Revealed* (New York: Owl Books, 2003).

32 This game was taught me by Rod Gnapp.

33 Johnstone, *Impro for Storytellers*, 285–301.

34 Robert Cohen, *Acting One*, 4th ed. (New York: McGraw-Hill, 2002), 41, 44.

35 The primary texts for this section are: Michael Chekhov, *To the Actor*; Chekhov, *On the Technique of Acting* (New York: HarperCollins, 1991); Franc Chamberlain, "Michael Chekhov on the Technique of Acting" from *Twentieth Century Actor Training*.

36 Mihaly Csikszentmihalyi, *Flow: The Psychology of Optimal Experience* (New York: Harper & Row, 1990).

37 Chekhov, *On the Technique of Acting*, 38.

38 Ibid., 28.

39 Ibid., 64.

40 Ibid., 89.

41 Hagen, *A Challenge for the Actor*, 194.

42 Foster Hirsch, *A Method to Their Madness: A History of the Actors Studio* (New York: W. W. Norton & Co., 1984), 150.

43 Ibid.

44 Gordon Rogoff, "Lee Strasberg: Burning Ice" from *Stanislavski and America*, 155.

45 Ibid., 167.

46 The primary sources for this section are: Erika Munk, ed., *Stanislavski and America*; Hirsch, *A Method to Their Madness*; David Krasner, "Strasberg, Adler and Meisner" from *Twentieth Century Actor Training*; Richard Brestoff, *The Great Acting Teachers and Their Methods* (Lyme, NH: Smith and Kraus, 1995); Cole, *Acting: A Handbook of the Stanislavski System*.

47 Richard Schechner, "Working with Live Material: An Interview with Lee Strasberg" from *Stanislavski and America*, 197.

48 Ibid., 187.

49 Hagen, *A Challenge for the Actor*, 98.

50 Richard Schechner, "Would You Please Talk to Those People?: An Interview with Robert Lewis" from *Stanislavski and America*, 232.

51 Cole, *Acting: A Handbook of the Stanislavski System*, 118.

52 Andre Belgrader, third-year acting class at the Yale School of Drama, 1986.

53 The primary sources for this section are: Meisner and Longwell, *Sanford Meisner on Acting*; Munk, *Stanislavski and America*; Krasner, "Strasberg, Adler and Meisner" from *Twentieth Century Actor Training*; Brestoff, *The Great Acting Teachers and Their Methods*.

54 Meisner and Longwell, *Sanford Meisner on Acting*, 16.

55 Ibid., 26.

56 Ibid., 34.

57 Ibid., 121.

58 Ibid., 81.

59 Ibid., 115.

60 Ibid., 73.

61 Ibid., 138.

62 Ibid., 96–97.

63 Ibid., 39.

64 Ibid., 40.

65 The primary sources for this section are: Peter Thomson, "Brecht and Actor Training" from *Twentieth Century Actor Training*; Willet, *Brecht on Theatre*; David Richard Jones, *Great Directors at Work: Stanislavsky, Brecht, Kazan, Brook* (Berkeley: University of California Press, 1986).

66 Willet, *Brecht on Theatre*, 22.

67 Ibid., 180.

68 Ibid., 188.

69 Ibid p.136

70 Thomson, "Brecht and Actor Training" from *Twentieth Century Actor Training*, 110.

71 Johnstone, *Impro for Storytellers*, 261.

72 Willet, *Brecht on Theatre*, 138.

73 John of Salisbury, *Metalogicon*, Daniel McGarry, trans. (New York: Peter Smith Publishers, 1985); http://en.wikipedia.org/wiki/Standing_on_the_shoulders_of_giants, Jan. 2007.

## 8  Other Voices

1 Adler, *The Technique of Acting*; www.pbs.org/wnet/americanmasters/database/adler_s.html, Jan. 2007; www.stellaadler.com/stella_adler.html, Jan. 2007.

2 www.alexandertechnique.com/fma.htm, Feb. 2007; http://en.wikipedia.org/wiki/ F. Matthias, Alexander, Feb. 2007.

3 www.theatrehistory.com/french/artaud001.html, Jan. 2007; http://en.wikipedia.org/wiki/Antonin_Artaud, Jan. 2007; www.antoninartaud.org/home.html, Jan. 2007.

4 http://www.ptoweb.org/about/boal.php, Jan. 2007; www.hno.harvard.edu/gazette/2003/12.11/15-boal.html, Jan. 2007.

5 http://www.siti.org/, Jan. 2007; http:// performance.tisch.nyu.edu/object/ps_alum_bogart.html, Jan. 2007; http://en.wikipedia.org/wiki/Viewpoints/, Jan. 2007.

6 Lorna Marshall and David Williams, "Peter Brook, Transparency and the Invisible Network" from *Twentieth Century Actor Training*; www.encyclopedia.com/doc/1E1-Brook-Pe.html, Jan. 2007.

7 www.amrep.org/people/bob.html, Jan. 2007; Robert Brustein, *Reimagining American Theatre* (New York: Hill and Wang, 1991).

8 John Rudlin, "Jacques Copeau: The Quest for Sincerity" from *Twentieth Century Actor Training*; http://en.wikipedia.org/wiki/Jacques_Copeau, Jan. 2007.

9 www.edge.org/3rd_culture/bios/foreman.html, Feb. 2007; www.brainy quote.com/quotes/authors/r/richard_foreman.html, Feb. 2007; Edwin Wilson and Alvin Goldfarb, *Theatre, the Lively Art* (New York: McGraw-Hill, 2006), 136.

10 Peter Brook, *The Empty Space* (New York: Touchstone, 1996), 59.

11 Lisa Wolford, "Grotowski's Vision of the Actor" from *Twentieth Century Actor Training*; Brestoff, *The Great Acting Teachers and Their Methods*; http://owendaly.com/jeff/grotows2.htm, Jan. 2007. Owen Daly, ed. www.culture.pl/en/culture/artykuly/os_grotowski_jerzy, Jan. 2007.

12 Hagen, *A Challenge for the Actor*; www.wic.org/bio/hagen.htm, Jan. 2007.

13 Johnstone, *Impro for Storytellers* (New York: Routledge, 1999) 283; www.laban.org/php/news.php?id=20, Feb. 2007; http://en.wikipedia .org/wiki/Laban_Movement_Analysis, Feb. 2007.

14 Robert Leach, "Meyerhold and Biomechanics," from *Twentieth Century Actor Training*; http://web.syr.edu/~kjbaum/aboutvsevolodmeyerhold .html, Jan. 2007; http://max.mmlc.northwestern.edu/~mdenner/Drama /directors/1meyerhold.html, Jan. 2007; http://en.wikipedia.org/ wiki/Vsevolod_Meyerhold, Jan. 2007.

15 Brestoff, *The Great Acting Teachers and Their Methods;* www.spolin.com/ violabio.html, Jan. 2007.

16 Brestoff, *The Great Acting Teachers and Their Methods;* www.blesok.com .mk/tekst.asp?lang=eng&tekst=484, Jan. 2007.

17 Brestoff, *The Great Acting Teachers and Their Methods,* 60–63; http://en.wikipedia.org/wiki/Vakhtangov_Theatre; Munk, *Stanislavski and America.*

18 Edwin Wilson and Alvin Goldfarb, *Living Theater* (McGraw-Hill: New York, 1994) 149; Lectures of Leon Katz, Yale School of Drama, 1983–1984.

19 www.livingtheatre.org/abou/history, Jan. 2007; Toby Cole and Helen Krich Chinoy, eds., *Actors on Acting* (New York: Crown, 1974), 652–3; www.villagevoice.com/theater/0328,feingold,45384,11.html, Jan. 2007; Hulton, Dornida, "Joseph Chaikin and Aspects of Actor Training" from *Twentieth Century Actor Training.*

## 9  Telling Classical Stories

1 *Henry V*, I, i, 17–18.

2 *Hamlet*, III, ii, 17–18.

3 This technique of Linklater's was used in classes with Linklater-certified teachers Zoe Alexander and Virginia Ness at the Yale School of Drama, 1985–1986 and Timothy Douglas, Chicago 1989.

4 This section is based on the lectures of David Perry of the Royal Academy of Dramatic Art London during a one-year course in London, 1981–1982, as well as the lectures of David Hammond of the Yale School of Drama from 1984–1985.

5 Brian Vickers, "Shakespeare's Use of Rhetoric" from *A New Companion to Shakespeare Studies*, Kenneth Muir and S. Schoenbaum, eds. (New York: Cambridge University Press, 1980), 84–88; http://en.wikipedia.org/wiki/Rhetoric, Jan. 2007.

6 Robert McCrum and Robert MacNeil, chapter 3 from *William Cran: The Story of English* (New York: Penguin Books, 2003).

7 This section is based on the lectures of David Perry of the Royal Academy of Dramatic Art London during a one-year course in London, 1981–1982.

8 *Hamlet*, III, ii, 4–8.

9 http://en.wikipedia.org/wiki/Shakespeare's_sonnets, Jan. 2007.

10 Johnstone, *Impro for Storytellers*, 23.

11 Ibid., 230

12 Ibid.

13 Ibid.

14 *Henry V*, I, i, 8–11.

15 *Richard III*, I, ii.

## 10  Telling New Stories

1 *Body Familiar* by Joe Goode, performed at the Magic Theatre, San Francisco, Calif., Dec. 16–Feb. 2, 2003.

## 11  Telling Stories: Where We Are Now

1 Stanislavski, *An Actor Prepares*, 192.

2 *Hamlet*, III, ii, 7–9.

# BIBLIOGRAPHY

## Acting and General Reference

Adler, Stella. *The Technique of Acting*. New York: Bantam Books, 1988.

Aristotle. *Poetics*. Kenneth McLeish, trans. New York: TCG, 1998.

Brestoff, Richard. *The Great Acting Teachers and Their Methods*. Lyme, NH: Smith and Kraus, 1995.

Brook, Peter. *The Empty Space*. New York: Touchstone, 1996.

———. *The Open Door*. New York, TCG, 1995.

Brustein, Robert. *Reimagining American Theatre*. New York: Hill and Wang, 1991.

Chaikin, Joseph. *The Presence of the Actor*. New York: Atheneum, 1984.

Cohen, Robert. *Acting One*. 4th ed. New York: McGraw-Hill, 2002.

Colo, Toby, and Helen Krich Chinoy, eds. *Actors on Acting*. New York: Crown, 1974.

Csikszetmihalyi, Mihaly. *Flow: The Psychology of Optimal Experience*. New York: Harper & Row, 1990.

Ekman, Paul. *Emotions Revealed*. New York, Owl Books, 2003.

Feynman, Richard P. *What Do You Care What Other People Think?* New York: W. W. Norton & Co., 1988.

Guskin, Harold. *How to Stop Acting*. New York: Faber & Faber, 2003.

Hagen, Uta. *Respect for Acting*. New York: McMillan, 1973.

———. *A Challenge for the Actor*. New York: Scribner, 1991.

Hodge, Alison, ed. *Twentieth Century Actor Training*. New York: Routledge, 2000.

Jones, David Richard. *Great Directors at Work: Stanislavsky, Brecht, Kazan, Brook*. Berkeley: University of California Press, 1986.

Keltner, Dacher. Psych 156, fall 2006, UC Berkeley Podcast, 2006, UC Regents.

Kleinman, Jim, ed. *The Best of PlayGround*. Six vols. San Francisco: PlayGround, 1997–2001, 2002, 2003, 2004, 2005, 2006.

Lane, Eric, and Nina Shengold. *Take Ten: New Ten-Minute Plays*. New York: Vintage, 1997.

———. *Take Ten II: More Ten-Minute Plays*. New York: Vintage, 2003.

Linklater, Kristin. *Freeing the Natural Voice*. New York: Drama Book Publishers, 1976.

Mamet, David. *True and False*. New York: Vintage Books 1997.

Moss, Larry. *The Intent to Live*. New York: Bantam Books, 2005.

Skinner, Edith. *Speak with Distinction*. New York: Applause, 1990.

Wilson, Edwin, and Alvin Goldfarb. *Living Theater*. New York: McGraw-Hill, 1994.

———. *Theatre, the Lively Art*. New York: McGraw-Hill, 2006.

## Improvisation and Theatre Games

Johnstone, Keith. *Impro*. New York, Routledge, 1992.

———. *Impro for Storytellers*. New York: Routledge, 1999.

## Stanislavski and the Moscow Art Theatre

Allen, David, and Jeff Fallow. *Stanislavski for Beginners*. New York: Writers and Readers Publishing, 1999.

Boleslavsky, Richard. *Acting: The First Six Lessons*. New York: Theatre Arts Books, 1949.

Cole, Toby, ed. *Acting: A Handbook of the Stanislavski System*. New York: Crown, 1979.

Stanislavski, Constantin. *An Actor's Handbook*. New York: Theatre Arts Books, 1963.

————. *An Actor Prepares*. New York: Theatre Arts Books, 1942.

————. *Building a Character*. New York: Theatre Arts Books, 1975.

————. *Creating a Role*. New York: Theatre Arts Books, 1978.

————. *My Life in Art*. New York: Theatre Arts Books, 1948.

## Brecht, Chekhov, Meisner, Strasberg

Chekhov, Michael. *Lessons for the Professional Actor*. New York: Performing Arts Journal Publications, 1985.

————. *On the Technique of Acting*. New York: HarperCollins, 1991.

————. *To the Actor*. New York: Perennial Library, 1985.

Hirsch, Foster. *A Method to Their Madness: A History of the Actors Studio*. New York: W. W. Norton & Co., 1984.

Meisner, Sanford, and Dennis Longwell. *Sanford Meisner on Acting*. New York: Vintage, 1987.

Munk, Erika, ed. *Stanislavski and America: "The Method" and Its Influence on the American Theatre*. (Greenwich, CT: Fawcett Premier, 1967.

Willet, John. *Brecht on Theatre*. New York: Hill and Wang, 1964.

## Shakespeare

Bloom, Harold. *Shakespeare: The Invention of the Human*. New York: Riverhead Books, 1998.

Brockbank, Philip, ed. *Players of Shakespeare 1*. New York: Cambridge University Press, 1985.

Crystal, David, and Ben Crystal. *The Shakespeare Miscellany*. New York: The Overlook Press, 2003.

Greenblatt, Stephen. *Will in the World*. New York: W. W. Norton, 2004.

Groom, Nick and Piero. *Introducing Shakespeare*. Lanham, MD: Totem Books, 2005.

Holden, Anthony. *William Shakespeare: The Man Behind the Genius*. New York: Little, Brown & Co., 1999.

Jackson, Russell, and Robert Smallwood. *Players of Shakespeare 2*. New York: Cambridge University Press, 1988.

Laroque, Francois. *The Age of Shakespeare*. New York: Harry N. Abrams Publishing, 1993.

Linklater, Kristin. *Freeing Shakespeare's Voice*. New York: TCG, 1992.

Marowitz, Charles. *The Other Way*. New York, Applause, 1999.

McCrum, Robert, and Robert MacNeil. *William Cran: The Story of English*. New York: Penguin Books, 2003.

Muir, Kenneth, and S. Schoenbaum, eds. *A New Companion to Shakespeare Studies*. (New York: Cambridge University Press, 1980.

Onions, C. T. *A Shakespeare Glossary*. New York: Oxford University Press, 1986.

*The Riverside Shakespeare*. Boston: Houghton Mifflin, 1974.

Tillyard, E. M. W. *The Elizabethan World Picture*. New York: Vintage, 1974.

Wood, Michael. *Shakespeare*. New York: Basic Books, 2003.

# Acknowledgments

Any book of this kind is by its nature a collaboration. I need to acknowledge the contributions made by many teachers, colleagues, and students to the elaboration and clarification of the methods and approaches here described. I also need to specifically thank Leon Katz, formerly of the Yale School of Drama, whose lectures from over twenty years ago formed the basis for the section on structure and whose wisdom is referenced throughout this book.

I also thank Keith Johnstone, whose workshops and writings provided a missing piece in my understanding of how to transmit the mechanics of live theatre in a joyful way. I also thank the late Dr. Maria Piscator for opening my eyes to an important period of history in which she played a part and the late Beatrice Straight, who provided firsthand knowledge of the techniques of Michael Chekhov.

This book was born out of experience, and I want to thank all of the actors whose process and work contributed to my understanding of acting. I would be remiss if I did not mention specific teachers and directors, David Perry, David Hammond, Earl Gister, Jim Barnhill, Zoe Alexander, Deborah Hecht, Andre Belgrader, Wesley Fata, Rey Buono, and Joe Goode who all shaped my thinking about acting. I also thank Peter Novak and the Performing Arts and Social Justice Department at the University of San Francisco for their encouragement and for providing me with a laboratory in which many of these techniques were tested.

I thank Marisa Smith and Erik Kraus who saw a possibility, and lastly, I would like to thank my family. I am grateful to my brother Mike who provided insight and to my eternally supportive mother Marjorie, who when faced with the news that not one but both of her sons were going into theatre, responded with grace and stoicism. I also thank my in-laws Lester and Unni Hoel for their support, as well as my sister-in-law Sonja and, of course, my children Tyler, Emma, and Jordan and my wife, Lisa, who is always my ultimate collaborator.

# ABOUT THE AUTHOR

Mark Rafael, an actor and educator, received his BA from Brown University and holds an MFA from the Yale School of Drama. He has also studied with teachers from the Royal Academy of Dramatic Art and the London Academy of Music and Dramatic Art in London and was awarded a scholarship to the Michael Chekhov Studio in New York. He served as an assistant to Dr. Maria Piscator, widow of Erwin Piscator, and has worked extensively on the development of new scripts in New York, Chicago, Los Angeles, and San Francisco. As an actor, he has performed in theatres across the country as well as in television and films, including James Cameron's *Titanic*. He currently lives and works in San Francisco with his wife and three children, where he teaches at the University of San Francisco and the Academy of Art University.